WELCOME TO MY
SANDBOX

WELCOME TO MY SANDBOX

JEANNE ALBERT

iUniverse LLC
Bloomington

WELCOME TO MY SANDBOX

Copyright © 2013 Jeanne Albert.

All rights reserved. No part of this book may be used or reproduced by any means, graphic, electronic, or mechanical, including photocopying, recording, taping or by any information storage retrieval system without the written permission of the publisher except in the case of brief quotations embodied in critical articles and reviews.

iUniverse books may be ordered through booksellers or by contacting:

iUniverse
1663 Liberty Drive
Bloomington, IN 47403
www.iuniverse.com
1-800-Authors (1-800-288-4677)

Because of the dynamic nature of the Internet, any web addresses or links contained in this book may have changed since publication and may no longer be valid. The views expressed in this work are solely those of the author and do not necessarily reflect the views of the publisher, and the publisher hereby disclaims any responsibility for them.

Any people depicted in stock imagery provided by Thinkstock are models, and such images are being used for illustrative purposes only. Certain stock imagery © Thinkstock.

ISBN: 978-1-4917-1004-3 (sc)
ISBN: 978-1-4917-1006-7 (e)

Library of Congress Control Number: 2013917654

Printed in the United States of America.

iUniverse rev. date: 10/17/2013

To Peter,

for your unending love and encouragement,

both in this life and beyond.

Contents

Preface xi
Introduction xvii

SANDBOX MONITORS 1
Hide Your Toys 3
What Goes Around 4
Be Careful What You Share 6
I Can Hear You 7
Want a Drink? 8
No Lunch for You! 9
E-mails and More E-mails 10
What's Your Name? 11
Just One More Question 12
Stating the Obvious 14
Spell Check 15
I Was Wrong 16
Who Is on the Phone? 17
Are You Looking at My . . . ? 18
Great Example 19
Chairs 101 21
Do You Know How to Spell? 22
Told You So 23
You Have No Clue 24
That's Not the Lesson 26
Others Can Hear You 27
Where's Your Uniform? 28
Termination Gone Wrong 29

King of the Jungle 32
It's All in the Details 33
Where's Waldo? 35
Taking Credit 36
A Quick Retort 37
At the Casino 38
Payback 39
You Don't Understand Us 42
We Value You 44

SANDBOX PLAYMATES **47**
It's a Good Idea, Right? 49
Halloween 50
Cut and Paste 51
Welcome Home 52
That's Not Funny 53
Voice Mail 54
Vanilla 55
Gotcha! 56
Did That Just Happen? 57
I Know 58
Wedgie 59
Dolls at Work 60
Leave a Message 61
Making an Entrance 62
Right Place, Right Time 64
Reply All 65
Al, Is That You? 66
Can I Have Your Cart? 67
I Know Where You Sit 68
Fire! 69

SANDBOX VISITORS **73**
Clams 75
What Are You Doing? 76
Character Reference 78
It Is a Sales Position 80
Who's First? 81
How Would You Handle It? 82
Now Be Nice 84
Bath Time 85
Please Don't Show Me 86
Watch Them! 87
My Girls 88
Milk Police 89
Thirteen and Important 91
Flowers and Lipstick 92
I'm Protected 94
I Am So Ready for This Job 95
Piss Off 96
A Dozen Doughnuts 97
Twenty-Five Cents 98
Thanks for Sharing 99
Uniform 100
I Don't Want to Shake Hands 101
Mix-Up 102
Merry Christmas 103
Wrestling 104
Get Back to Work 105
What Are You Looking At? 106
Nice Doggy 108
Give Us a Hug 109
Garage Door 110
Best Friends 112
Did You Just Ask Me That? 113
Can I Go Now? 114

Who Took My Shoes? 116
What's Wrong with That? 117
Temps 120
The Judge 121
I Did Not Know That 122
Green Men 123

Conclusion 125

Preface

"Connecting the world, one funny story at a time."

My first "job" was an entrepreneurial adventure with the eight-year-old girl who lived next door to my grandmother. We decided we were going to be millionaire lemonade-stand operators on a quiet street in suburbia. After much debate as to who was going to purchase—or should I say, *pilfer*—the ingredients from home, we set up our little booth. I don't think we were five minutes into our endeavor when this young girl and I got into an argument. She stormed away, declaring to the world that she *hated my guts*! Well, I had never heard that term before, and when I approached my grandmother with my inquiry, she responded by saying it was slang for someone's insides.

I thought about this, and in my youth and innocence, I replied, "But how can she hate them when she can't even see them?" And so started my many adventures and experiences at work!

I've always had a love of stories—hearing them, creating them, and sharing them. My brother and I used to create stories about people walking by in the airport while we waited to board a plane to our grandfather's house.

"That guy is an international spy, and his briefcase has top-secret papers in it," I would say.

And my brother would add, "She's a kung fu master on her way to train someone."

The tales got wilder by the minute and usually ended up in peals of laughter! Despite our rough upbringing, we always managed to use humor to find a way through.

The day I found out that my brother had decided to leave us was the beginning of a new life for me. My whole world changed. People often talk about loss and use eloquent words to describe what they feel, but for me, one minute I was living my life and the next, the path had literally dissolved from under me. Most days, I felt I was in a play for which I had not been given a script. I simply had to figure it out as I went along.

I know that what he chose to do had not been an easy decision. I know that he had fought with depression most of his life, and I'm only now beginning to understand how he felt. His constant battle reminds me of a story I once heard:

> *Many years ago, an old Cherokee grandfather decided it was time to take his grandson for a serious talk. As they reached the crest of a hill and looked down upon the valley, the grandfather began to tell a story once told to him by his own grandfather. He said: "Inside every one of us is a Good Wolf and a Bad Wolf. We have no choice about it. Both are within us at birth. However, as we grow up and become adults in life, one of these wolves will kill the other wolf and then dominate our lives and the way we treat others."*
>
> *The young Cherokee child looked at his grandfather and asked, "But Grandfather, how will I know which wolf will win the fight?"*
>
> *The grandfather smiled and said, "That is quite simple to know. The wolf that will win the fight is the one you feed the most."*

I now understand the term *labor of love*. The task of writing this book was that and more. When I set out to pay tribute to my brother, I began with an idea. I worked diligently with a coach for a year, but after several starts—but mostly stops—I decided to walk away from that project. I was devastated, as I thought I had truly found something that would properly honor him. I then began another venture that fizzled out, this one after only six months. At a loss and feeling very frustrated, I told my partner I was going to stop trying and that if it were meant to be, an idea would come to me. A few days after making that statement, I got the idea for the book you now hold in your hand. It began originally as an exercise I gave to my students when I taught recruitment and selection at a local college. The exercise was to share weird business situations they had experienced and to explore together how they could have been handled from a human resources (HR) perspective. My *aha* moment came when I remembered my brother's laugh, believe it or not. It was the kind that made you laugh along just hearing it, even if you hadn't heard the reason for it, or the joke. Then I remembered how we had always loved to share stories, especially those centered on our work experiences. It was at that moment that the tribute and the idea for the book came together. I knew I was onto something because—unlike the other projects—this one flowed, and help in many forms facilitated the process. That's not to say that it wasn't a challenging undertaking. Quite the contrary! In writing this book, I learned a great deal not only about myself but also about others.

Most of the stories are from friends, colleagues, and family, and some are from my own personal experiences. As a twenty-five-year-plus veteran of the HR profession, I've met my fair share of naysayers. I have never condoned malicious or harassing behavior, but I have also learned that it's not personal at all; toxic coworkers have many deep-seated personal issues that they need to sort through. I've never seen or worked in a workplace that didn't have some kind of problems. However, fostering a fun environment built on trust and respect can go a long way toward impacting the mental health of everyone who works there, not to mention the financial bottom line. We have to remember that a culture is *created*, not mandated; frankly, nothing sucks the fun out of things more than a policy that seeks to control a workplace environment. If nothing else, perhaps this is an opportunity to examine your own "sandbox." What do you see? Is it a "work happy" environment?

I realize that organizations still have a long way to go in terms of engaging their employees through laughter and meaningful working environments. Work and fun do not have to be mutually exclusive. Research continues to prove that we are more creative and innovative when we work in a fun environment. Isn't this what we need in our society—to not only be competitive on a global scale, but also to lessen the effects that toxic environments have on us all?

"At the height of laughter, the universe is flung into a kaleidoscope of new possibilities" (Jean Houston).

Not long ago, I read this quotation and it moved me deeply. The fact is that we all need to laugh more—at ourselves and at the world around us. In the exact moment we share laughter, we feel understood and connected. It doesn't matter where we come from, or what constitutes our background or experiences. We all have to work for a living, and sharing our "sandbox stories" is a powerful connector.

This book not only honors my brother's love of laughter and stories, but also allows people to connect through laughter and makes it possible to impact mental health, since a portion of the proceeds from the book sales will be donated to mental health charities.

I believe that ideas are much like seeds; they need the right kind of environment, the proper care, and sufficient encouragement to grow and be fruitful. This book is the result of so many people, and I would like to take the time to acknowledge them:

I would first like to thank my father for always being my biggest fan. Long ago, I wrote: "Once upon a time there was a bear and a rabbit, they did not like each other, they did not do jokes together." Who would have thought that a writer could have grown from these humble beginnings? Thanks for keeping my first story on the back of your checkbook. I love you, Dad.

To my beautiful children, Kai and Kyana: Your influence over me is undeniable, unquestionable, and unbelievable. You are little treasures over whom God has chosen me to watch. I will always love and take care of you, and I hope I'll always be deserving of your love.

I would like to thank you, Nick, for being such a great father and the best ex a partner could ever ask or hope for.

To my best friend, Janice—my soul sister: They say that a true friend reflects back all that is good in us, but also makes us face that which we don't care for in order to help us grow. Well, my friend, you are a true and genuine mirror to me and I love you.

To my "twin flame," Geoff: I would wait another lifetime and go through everything all over again to be with you. You mirror my best qualities and complete my heart. I love you.

To my mother, for all that we have shared and continue to share—thank you for being my other biggest fan!

To Jane, Moira, and Heidi: You are amazing women, and I am blessed by your support, encouragement, and laughter!

To Sabaina, Andrew, Rania, and Kristof: Thank you for being patient, kind, beyond generous, supportive, and understanding—and for making this project part of your own hearts.

To the amazing team at iUniverse: Thank you for your guidance and for making the process of publishing so easy, seamless, and—dare I say—fun!

To my friends, colleagues, coaches, students, and clients, and anyone else with whom I have crossed paths and who has left an indelible mark on my life: There are too many of you to name here, but please know that you have influenced me and that I thank you for your support and encouragement, and everything in between. I am truly blessed!

I would like to thank my brother for being there for me through thick and thin, and at every point in between. Thank you for overlooking the mistakes I have made and always seeing and rejoicing in my triumphs. I could not have asked or prayed for a nicer brother. I know you have been with me every step of this journey—even now, when you are no longer with us physically.

To everyone who contributed stories: Thank you from the bottom of my heart for being so willing to share your experiences with me. Know that—with your help—we are making a difference in the world.

With love and light,
Jeanne

Introduction

Ever wondered if others encounter funny and weird situations at work just like you do? Wonder no more!

Welcome to my Sandbox is a collection of stories that center on the funny and sometimes weird stuff that happens to us at work. Regardless of the job, we all have stories we share with our friends and family that start with: "You'll never guess what happened to me at work today!" These stories make us either laugh or shake our heads in disbelief, yet they unite us because, after all, "Everybody laughs the same in every language because laughter is a universal connection" (Y. Smirnoff).

Whether they involve a boss (Sandbox Monitor), a coworker (Sandbox Playmate), or customers (Sandbox Visitors), the stories contained here recount real-life experiences from a wide variety of people across a multitude of industries and backgrounds.

Since we spend the vast majority of our day playing in a sandbox with others, it's no surprise that misadventures happen!

People's names throughout this book have been changed. While the stories were edited for grammar, the voice of the storyteller was kept intact.

SANDBOX MONITORS

I was once told that teachers come in all different forms, and I have to agree. Everyone in our lives has the ability to teach us, and this is especially true of our bosses. Some, endowed with virtues and leadership skills, inspire us to emulate them. Others teach us by demonstrating what *not* to do. Both types shape and form us.

Many of the stories in this book reflect my own experiences; others were submitted by colleagues, friends, or family and business associates. Many times, the stories I received began with, "You'll never believe this happened to me." After the stories were shared, I always asked, "Did you learn anything from the experience?" The answers were very telling; not one person said "no"!

I'm sure that, as you read through the stories, you'll laugh or shake your head in disbelief. Either way, though, you'll be entertained and offered encouragement if you're facing similar difficult situations involving *your* boss!

Hide Your Toys

I work for a woman who runs a consulting business out of her home. She has two small children who, on occasion, are there when I am. One day, my boss asked one of her children to go upstairs to retrieve something out of her bathroom. Well, her child went upstairs for a moment and returned holding a vibrator. He then looked at both of us and, with it vibrating in his hand, asked, "What's *this*, Mommy?"

What Goes Around

After graduating from university with a degree in journalism, I arrived in Toronto from Montreal, bright-eyed and bushy-tailed, wanting that perfect starter job in news media. I soon landed a job with one of the prominent advertising companies in Toronto. The only opening they had was for an understudy to one of the top advertising executives, so I was basically there to learn from him. Long story short, he said that I was "no understudy" and invited me to go to Italy with him. I was twenty-five years old and he was much, much older than me. I said no and he fired me. I was devastated because I had no family in Toronto and now no job. So I went to an employment agency and they ended up hiring me. God only knows why they took a chance on me, because I really didn't have a lot of confidence, but they took me on while I looked for another job—and the position paid a really good salary.

Isn't fate an amazing thing? I ended up staying in the field and getting my designation. I was doing really well as a recruiter, and because of my background in journalism and my knowledge about agencies and marketing, I created a great reputation for myself. One day, I picked up a job order with a different employment agency and was invited to meet with the person I would be assisting in finding a "right-hand person." This was a big deal, and as I sat in the boardroom with the management team, in walked the same guy who had fired me! He was the guy I would be doing the search for!

You can only imagine how, as he walked in, he took one look at me and—I swear—turned red from the top of his balding head to his toes. He started looking around the room and trying to speak, but he couldn't get any words out. Everyone was looking at him and wondering what was going on. To say he was not composed would be an understatement. As he sat down, he stared at his notes. He was so angry, humiliated, and embarrassed because he had to work with me, and I was on retainer.

This, of all the incidents in my life, was the event that I most remember as being a classic example of *payback*. In fact, it was payback in a big-time way, because he had to work with me, speak with me, be cooperative with me, and be there during the interviews with me. And he was furious the whole time. He kept trying to find ways to get rid of me, but I did such a great job of finding someone that he had no recourse but to accept my presence.

Finally, after he hired the girl I found, he called me and said, "You must have really been enjoying this."

And I said, "Actually, yes, I was. And by the way, if *anything* happens to the woman I placed with you (as she was not exactly a dog)—if she loses that job for any reason other than work performance—I *will say* something."

Be Careful What You Share

When I first moved from my hometown to Toronto, I was pretty immature and naïve. I rented a room in a house where the owner lived as well. He was a big control freak who also tried to seduce all the girls who lived there. One day he got drunk during a house party and divulged that he had two of everything "down there." Of course, he was drinking and none of us believed it.

I left on bad terms a couple of months later, because some stuff had been stolen from my bedroom—personal stuff that I had brought with me (my grandmother's china, and so forth)—and I really thought the owner was the thief, as he alone had access to the rooms that were kept under lock and key.

Three or four years went by. I was working in the recruiting field and who walked in for an interview one day? The guy! He took one look at me, recognized me, and was immediately embarrassed. I started interviewing him and he stood up.

"Listen, I know there is no way you're going to hire me, so don't waste my time. And if you ever tell anyone that I have two penises, I will kill you," he said.

What he didn't realize until a few moments later was that the door to the interview room had been open—with a bullpen of my colleagues sitting behind the door! Essentially, *everyone* in the office had heard his outburst! So I looked at him and then moved my gaze behind him, and this is when he realized what he had done. People were staring at him; even people on the phone were sitting there with their mouths open. I didn't know how he would react. He grabbed his stuff and stormed out of the office. Right after he left, everyone in the office howled and, of course, asked me how *I* knew what he had down there!

I Can Hear You

During an interview for a sales manager position, the hiring manager started raising his voice to me—asking me questions such as: "*Why do you think you would fit this role?*" My first reaction was to look for the hidden camera, but I thought twice about it when I noticed the look on his face. So I calmly replied that I felt I was best suited for the role because of my background and qualifications, and so forth. "*No!*" he yelled back. "*Why the hell should we hire you?*" This time he was only inches from my face, at which point I looked him straight in the eye and said, "It is not necessary for you to scream at me; I can hear you just fine." He then smiled, pulled away, and said with a laugh, "That is my way of seeing if you can handle stressful situations." I got up, picked up my things, and told him there were *other* ways of determining if I could handle stress—and this wasn't one of them.

Want a Drink?

I interviewed and ultimately went to work for one of the most off-the-wall bosses. When I went into my first interview with him, he asked me what I thought of my field, why I had gotten into it, and so on. Those were the only questions he asked. After that, he walked over to the fridge and got a beer. He offered me one, but I refused as (a) I do not drink beer, and I wanted to make a good impression, and (b), even if I did, it was only eleven in the morning!

No Lunch for You!

I once worked for a company president who had a really different take on employee relations. I had befriended his administrative assistant, and several weeks after I started, we decided to join a local gym. Since the gym was only about a two-minute walk from the office, we thought we could work out, grab something to eat, and alter our schedules by staying a bit later on the days we went to the gym. Perfect, right? Two days later, the president pulled his assistant into his office and in no uncertain terms told her that she could not work out on her lunch hour. He then told her that he greatly admired the office manager because she didn't take any breaks and ate lunch at her desk. That same afternoon, I got a call from my boss telling me in softer terms that we needed to be the ones to set the standards for the company and that the president had his quirks; this was just one of them. The next day I met with the president on a totally different matter. He started in saying he wanted to talk to me about this lunch-hour thing. I told him that my boss had already had this conversation with me, but he insisted on sharing his views on the situation. He said he felt that lunches were for wimps and (just like his father before him) he shared that same philosophy. He said that if he had his druthers, he would ban them altogether! Then he started extolling the virtues of the office manager who would take fifteen minutes to run (and he waved his arms when explaining this to me) to get a sandwich and then run back to the office so that she wouldn't miss a call!

E-mails and More E-mails

It was my second day on the job when my boss approached me in the hallway to ask a question. Now, my boss never got the memo on the concept of personal space, since he (as I later found out) would get inches away from your face to discuss things with you. Add to this the fact that he smoked and drank coffee heavily throughout the day, and you can imagine his breath; to say it was putrid would be an understatement.

So his question—more of a command, actually—to me on that particular morning was, "I want to see your e-mails before you send them out."

I looked at him askance and indicated that I didn't understand what he meant.

He explained, "I need to see all of your e-mails so I can determine the way you write."

I was flabbergasted and said, "Is that not something you should have determined prior to hiring me? I've been in a senior position for five years and have written communications to senior-level executives for years before that."

"No matter," he said, waving me off. "I want to see *all* of them."

So over the next two days I copied him on all of my e-mails—and I do mean *all* of them. I sat in my office and did nothing but compose e-mails to everyone in the company, as well as external contacts, and so forth. This was easy to do as we had locations all over Canada and the United States. After the second day, he popped into my office and told me it was okay to stop sending him e-mails, as he approved of the way I wrote them and—to be honest, he added—the sheer volume of them had overwhelmed him. It turned out that it was a good thing after all; when I met with the senior executives in our remote offices, they said how nice it was that I had taken the time to e-mail them personal messages!

What's Your Name?

I had only been on the job for about three days at a firm downtown, and I needed to speak with my boss about some candidates we were planning on bringing in for interviews. So I met with him and proceeded to go through the names and highlights for each candidate. He then turned to me and started off on a tirade about a particular race and how he once hired someone from that background and *blah, blah, blah*. He went on for about five minutes, and as he was talking, I was thinking, *Gosh, I must be on* Candid Camera *and someone is going to pop out and say, "Surprise!" because this surely isn't happening!* But he was for real. The most asinine part is that, when he hired me, he would have gathered from my hyphenated last name that I am interracially married to a man of that same race!

Just One More Question

I got a call from someone asking me to come for an interview at a very prestigious bank in Chicago. I jumped at the chance and was booked for an interview the next day. When I arrived at the bank's address, there were no cars in the parking lot, which I thought was kind of weird, and when I walked into the facility, it looked like a bomb had gone off in it. I looked around for anyone and saw someone approaching from the far corner of the building. She turned out to be the hiring manager, and she explained that they were going through extensive renovations and that—when finished—it would look quite nice. She then led me to her office and gave me a quick overview of the interview process and proceeded to pull out what appeared to be a small phone book. She must have caught the look on my face, because she smiled and said, "I believe in extensive interviewing and probing." I gave a nervous smile in response, and she began asking me behavioral-based questions.

At about the hour mark her assistant knocked and said she had a call, to which she waved her off. About ten minutes later I asked if I could please have a glass of water. Her reply? "We are almost finished with the questions, and could you please wait until then?" Not wanting to appear pushy, I conceded—thinking that it was almost over. Well, forty-five minutes later I told her I needed to use the facilities, and I stood up while asking. She said, "Of course," and opened her door, showing me the hallway that led to the bathroom. I brought my purse, and as I walked toward the bathroom, I happened to glance over and saw an exit door with my car parked outside. To this day I don't know what possessed me to do this—maybe it was the thought of being trapped in that office answering questions until I was brain dead. After I came out of the bathroom, I pushed the door and made a run for my car. I was just at my car door when I heard her assistant calling to me, but I pretended I couldn't hear her and peeled out of the parking lot. I called my husband on the way home, and he asked how the interview went. When I told him what I had done, he asked me to clarify—so I told him I had bolted! It doesn't end there! Imagine my surprise two days later when I get a call from her assistant letting me know that the hiring manager was really impressed with me and wanted me to come back in and finish the interview . . . *Hello?*

Stating the Obvious

I was working for a large bakery firm and was about to finalize the details of my permanent transfer to the US division. During a staff meeting, my (about-to-be-former) boss asked a bunch of questions about the position that I had accepted, what I knew about my new boss, and so forth. At the end of this discussion, he turned to me in front of my peers.

"You know, the only reason you are going is that he wants you," he announced.

Talk about an awkward silence as we all looked at one another.

Spell Check

I was working on a national project where I had to give updates on a regular basis to the vice presidents, board members, and CEO of the company. When the project was finished, I wrote a final e-mail summarizing what had been done, the roadblocks we had encountered, and the benefits to expect from the changes we had implemented. As it was a lengthy e-mail, I read it, reread it, and finally did a spell check to make sure it was absolutely perfect—since it was going to the top people in the company and any mistake would be unacceptable. It was perfect! I hit send feeling so confident and proud for having facilitated a successful project. Five minutes later, I got an e-mail from my boss. I opened it, thinking he was going to congratulate me on a job well done. I was *sooo* wrong. He pointed out how at the end of my e-mail, where I should have written, "Regards," I wrote instead, "Retards." Moral of this story: *never trust spell check!*

I Was Wrong

We all used to eat lunch together in the boardroom—the staff and our boss. Just so you have some background, our boss never liked to admit he was wrong in anything. One day, he was telling us how much he and his wife enjoyed stage plays (he more so than her) and especially *La Bohème*, which he pronounced "bo-HEEM."

I piped up and said, "I think you mean *La Bohème*, pronounced *bo-EM*."

"No," he answered. "It's *La Bo-HEEM*, and I bet you five dollars that I'm right."

"Okay," I answered.

I didn't hear anything about it until about a week later when he approached me and said, "I just want to let you know that I have your five dollars and that you were right—it's *La Bo-EM*."

And I said, "You can keep the five dollars; you admitting that you were wrong is worth the five dollars." I don't think he liked that very much, as he stormed off.

Who Is on the Phone?

When I was working in the car rental business, our company filed for bankruptcy protection and as a result stopped paying many of our bills. One of the top two motor companies contacted us about unpaid bills. Our controller, who wasn't the sharpest knife in the drawer, yelled, "Screw (the name of another company)! Who the hell are they to tell us we have to pay them?" My only thoughts were, *Well, we are a car rental company, and _____ is only the number-two car manufacturer in the world. I guess they are not important to us . . .*

Are You Looking at My . . . ?

I went into my boss's office for my annual performance review. It happened to be a casual day, so I had on blue jeans and a somewhat loose-fitting, plain, white, long-sleeved T-shirt. This becomes important later.

I sat down in the chair, and things were going very well—it was very casual. Then out of nowhere my boss (who obviously didn't have that much experience or education in conducting performance reviews) told me that although he liked my breasts, he would never stare at them at work because that wouldn't be appropriate. He proceeded to tell me that if we were out at a bar he *would* look, though! I was now painfully aware of my white shirt and immediately covered myself up with the papers I had in my hands.

I diverted the conversation back to my review, and we got to the next section. All the while I was thinking what an idiot he was and wanting the review to be over. A couple of sections later he came to the section titled "Personal Growth." He snickered and looked at me with a sly grin, focusing his eyes on my bottom half. I couldn't help myself, and I asked, "Are you commenting on the size of my ass?" Unbelievably, his reply was, "Don't worry—your husband has gained weight too. All newly married people do." Well, I quickly wrapped up the review, stood up, and walked out of his office, trying to muster as much dignity as I could and thinking, *Too bad I didn't have any paper I could cover my apparently large butt with too!*

Great Example

I once interviewed for a director role at a local health-care facility. I showed up at the appointed hour only to find the double glass doors locked. I peered in and luckily someone walked by. She came up to the door and mouthed, "What do you want?" I replied that I had an interview scheduled. She proceeded to let me in and told me to sign in on the sheet and that someone would be with me shortly. I sat opposite the boardroom and heard peals of laughter. That went on for about ten minutes while I sat waiting. Finally the door opened, and the candidate—along with the hiring manager—stepped out. They shook hands, and the manager patted the candidate on the back and led him off down the hallway. A women looked at me and said, "We'll be right with you." She shut the door, another ten minutes rolled by, and finally the door opened again; I was motioned to come in. I stepped in and stood there with my coat waiting for instructions on where to sit. They were all busy chatting and filling in their notes, so I picked a chair and put my coat on the chair next to me. There were three people in the room. All of them had glasses of water in front of them, and there was a big jug of water—but I wasn't offered any. Brief introductions were made and the interview began. The hiring manager asked me seventeen situational questions, such as: *We have a problem with such and such; how would you go about solving it?* These were no ordinary problems. They were complex, and I often needed to ask them to elaborate on the information they were providing. Meanwhile, they were busy writing stuff down and probing me about why I would do something a certain way. I got the sneaking suspicion that there really wasn't a position available, but that this was just a guise to figure out different solutions to their problems. After an hour and a half, the hiring manager looked up, exasperated that she couldn't seem to get to all seventeen questions in the time allotted. They asked if I had any questions for them, and I asked one of the assistants something, but the hiring manager interrupted her and answered on her behalf. Oh, and did I mention that the whole time during the interview the hiring manager was chewing gum? After the interview, they walked me to the glass doors where we engaged in an impromptu conversation in which I told her that I taught recruitment and selection at a local college and I would be using this experience as an example for my next class. The look on her face was priceless. They called about a week later, asking me to come back in for another interview. I declined.

Chairs 101

"You've gotta be kidding! You mean I have to give a course on sitting on *chairs*?" I asked.

The background here is that there was an executive who sat on a four-legged stool chair and used to like to lean back on it. One day, he was laughing, leaned back too far, and fell right off—*right* at the time the safety committee was walking by.

"Oh my God—that's a safety incident!" they said, and it came down from the president later that day that all health and safety committees had to give a thirty-minute lecture on the proper way to sit on chairs.

Later, in my boss's office, I piped up and asked, "This is a joke, right? How on earth can I give a thirty-minute talk about sitting on chairs?"

And he answered, "I don't care, but the president said you have to do it."

So we convened the entire group with the safety committee, and I had to give a thirty-minute talk on the proper way to sit on chairs, as well as the differences between four-legged and three-legged stools. After that, the company gave the chairs away (and these were expensive company executive chairs) to the United Way for five dollars a pop.

We were scratching our heads over this whole ordeal when—I swear to God, no word of a lie—the next day, Dilbert came out with a cartoon on how to sit properly in a chair. And I said, "Holy crap, there's a bug in here—Dilbert works here!"

Do You Know How to Spell?

I had an interview for a sales position at a fairly well-known bakery. It had taken about two weeks of coordinating with the manager to figure out when I could come in, and she sounded great over the phone. I felt that we would hit it off just as well in person.

Well, as I waited for my interview, some gentleman—and I use the term in its loosest form—came in to the reception area and started bragging about his new car. Now, by *bragging* I don't mean just talking, but being a loud, obnoxious character. I could see everyone's negative reaction to him. To boot, he wore a really bad hairpiece. In the back of my mind I was thinking, *What a jerk—good thing I'm not interviewing with him.*

Well, I shouldn't have assumed this too soon! You guessed it; I got called into the boardroom, and the manager informed me that this was going to be my direct supervisor and that is why he was in the interview. Aside from being a jerk, he proceeded to ask me virtually every illegal question in the book, like: "Are you going to get married?" and "Have kids?" He also had me run though a battery of tests, one of which was spelling.

I didn't hear back from this company until about two weeks later, when I received a letter in the mail stating that I didn't get the job. Oh, and did I mention the letter addressed from him had three spelling mistakes? I wish I had sent it back to them, but it was the company my father worked for, and I knew that word would get back to him!

Told You So

We were interviewing for a VP position at a company I worked for, and three candidates had been sent to us to interview. The first person was good, but didn't have half of the qualities we were looking for. The next person was fantastic, had a presentation for us, and had all of the prerequisite skills we were looking for. The third person was, I swear, a modern version of Herb Tarlic from WKRP. He wore a bad suit, had bad hair, and was even worse in answering *any* of the questions posed to him. I kept asking him what he had done in the past, and he kept answering what he *would* do. After about forty-five frustrating minutes, I ended the interview, letting him know we would be in touch.

After he left, my boss bounded into the office and asked, "What do you think?" *What did I think?* I told him frankly and openly what my thoughts were, to which he replied, "Well, thanks for your opinion, but I've already decided on the last guy." As my boss walked out of my office, my jaw was still on the floor.

But, oh, it gets better! So we hired this individual, and at the next big industry event he got drunk, paraded around with two hookers, and then told everyone the next morning how he had run out of money and had to go downstairs to the ATM machine so he could continue having fun with *the girls*. Every time I think of this story, I'm reminded of a famous MasterCard commercial. In this guy's case, the script would have gone: *Damage to company? Priceless!*

You Have No Clue

Until the fall of 2012, I worked as an independent contractor for the Canadian licensee of a behavioral assessment tool. I had started with the guy because I had been looking for an opportunity that would afford me both independence and the ability to build a recurring income stream. As it turned out, I ended up with no independence and a licensee who made it *very clear* who owned the revenue stream.

For the last three years that I was associated with this boss, we would get into a running battle every spring. This coincided with the start of the last quarter of his fiscal year. The more he would try to tighten the screws, the more I would react—a predictable result he should have been aware of had he paid any attention to my behavioral profile! What was it that we were selling again?

By March 2012, we were at rock bottom from a relationship perspective, and I made the decision that we would have to part ways. The problem was that I had opportunities in the works that I wouldn't get paid for if I just walked away. I was pretty sure—based on his demeanor and some e-mails that he had shared with me—that he was getting ready to fire me. So I implemented what I began to call "the great runway extension project of 2012."

The first step of this project was a face-to-face meeting with Ron (whose name I've changed) in which we "kissed and made up." Part of the process was getting him to believe that I was back onside and fully engaged, so I played what another colleague called the Super Duper Great Guns with my boss until I eventually told him I was done. This involved being positive, upbeat, and never sharing a discouraging word. The problem, as a leader, is that you get no usable information when the people who work for you are forced to play games.

I qualified for the President's Club award and won a trip for two to New York City. All the while, I continued to keep the runway extension project going. Just prior to the trip to NYC, my boss sent me an e-mail with the subject line, "Thank you for your hard work this year," and proceeded to tell me how proud he was that I had sucked it up and begun to toe the line with him. (He didn't use those words, but that was the intent.) The fact is that I didn't give a rat's behind whether he was proud of me or not. When you have no respect for someone, you couldn't care less about what they think about you.

I decided to respond to Ron's e-mail as follows: "You're welcome. You have no idea how this makes me feel."

I was really just stating the fact that I knew he had no clue how little his message meant to me. The beauty of *double entendre*, as well as his predictability, however, is that he read it differently. His response? "Good to hear. Have a great last week of our sales year."

When the runway ran out in October 2012, he never saw it coming. And everything that he has done since I pulled the plug on our relationship confirms that getting clear of him was the right thing to do.

That's Not the Lesson

I remember walking past my boss's office one day; he had his door open and was yelling at one of his subordinates. Later on, I walked into his office and politely suggested that in the future he might want to shut his door when reprimanding his employees. He replied, "I think it's important to let others in the office hear this. That way they understand the consequences for making errors and that sloppiness won't be tolerated."

Others Can Hear You

I was looking for work and made my rounds at various staffing agencies. One of them sticks out in my mind as being the weirdest. I walked in and told the receptionist that I was there for an appointment. She handed me a clipboard to fill out, and we started chatting. I discovered that she spoke my native language, so we started conversing in it. All of a sudden, a door burst open and two women, arguing and swearing at each other, crossed the lobby, went through another door, and slammed it shut.

I looked up at the receptionist, and she shrugged her shoulders and rolled her eyes at me. I was just about to finish my application and was about to stand up when I heard the door rush open and the two women going at it again—this time louder and with more obscene language. When they finally crossed the lobby and slammed another door shut behind them, I look at the receptionist and—in our native language—asked if this was a regular occurrence.

She smiled and nodded her head. I gave her back the clipboard and took the app, ripped it up, and told her to put it in the garbage. She smiled and replied, "I don't blame you."

Where's Your Uniform?

As a manager of a local fast-food chain, I often have to deal with young kids and their first jobs, and inevitably issues around responsibility. I once had a young man report to work with only half of his uniform on. When I asked him what happened to the other half, he replied that his Mom hadn't finished doing the laundry. So I walked him to the office, where I proceeded to pull out his application and ask him who signed off on it. He sheepishly said himself. "So," I said, "you agreed to be responsible for this job, right? And not your Mom?" He nodded. I told him that he had two choices: he could either go home and stay there, or he could come back fully clothed and ready to work. We never had another issue with laundry again!

Termination Gone Wrong

The decision was made to fire the president. My boss, the vice president of human resources, came into my office to discuss the details of when it would go down and how best to approach the matter. I thought it best to terminate her after everyone went home, but my boss thought it might be better to do it just before lunch. So on the day of the deed, he proceeded with the termination meeting with the president. After lunch, I stopped by his office to ask him how it went.

He said, "Great. She really handled it well."

Wow, that's fantastic, I thought. *Terminations are usually very hard on all parties involved.* "So where is she now?" I asked.

"In her office," he answered. "She said she needed time to clear out her things."

Now, in termination meetings, you can offer the people being terminated some time to clear out their belongings—as typically it's embarrassing for them to have to walk out of the office in front of their peers or employees with their personal effects in hand. So I was surprised that he had not arranged for her to come back at a later time. *Oh well,* I thought. *He seems to have it under control, and he is my boss, after all.*

The next day, imagine my surprise when I swiped my elevator card on the parking level and stepped in, only to have it open on the first floor of the building and have the president walk in, say "good morning," and then punch in our floor. The whole time I was thinking, *What's going on?* I tried to put on the best poker face I could muster. She walked toward her office. Before I could get a chance to speak with my boss, however, my assistant called me into her office to discuss a performance problem with another employee.

My whole day escaped me, and I left to avoid getting caught in rush-hour traffic. The next morning I was in my office sipping coffee, and my boss came in, sweating profusely; he seemed nervous and quite agitated. I asked him what was wrong, and he responded by saying that the president still hadn't left.

"What do you mean?" I asked.

"I mean, she hasn't *left*," he replied. "She keeps coming back day after day, and I don't know what to do."

For a brief moment, I thought, *So remind me again why you're my boss and I'm your subordinate?* "Okay," I told him. "It's simple; we have passkeys to get up into the elevator, right?"

"Yes," he said with a nod.

"Okay, so have security block her access once she goes out for lunch. Have her secretary alert you, but first speak with security and let them know to be on standby. Then, have her secretary source out a shipping company that can come in and clear out her personal effects and have them couriered to her house. Call her house and either speak with her in person or leave a message indicating that her personal effects will be shipped at X time."

"Okay," he said, rushing out of my office.

I later found out through his secretary that he had basically left all of those instructions with her and she was the one who had handled them, exactly as I had suggested.

But, oh, it only gets better. So we were now in negotiations with the said president because—in my boss's earlier rush to get her on board—he had not gotten a proper offer letter together, and there were no terms and conditions for her termination. Three days later, my boss asked me to accompany him to a meeting with the recruitment firm that had provided us with the president. We met at this incredibly expensive restaurant downtown. The owner of the firm told us how reputable his firm was and how thorough they were in sourcing out candidates, and so forth. After hearing these *songs in the key of me* for about ten minutes, I politely interjected with some questions.

"So what kinds of tests did you perform on the candidate?" I asked.

"Well," he said, "we did an in-basket test." (For those of you who may not know this, it tests how well someone can prioritize their work based on the information contained in the in-basket.)

"So," I asked, "what else?"

"Well, aside from our interviews, which are incredibly thorough, we find that this kind of testing tells us a lot about the person."

In the back of my mind I was thinking, *And you charged us huge fees for that? Okay, surely you did background checks.* So I asked about this, but they replied, "No. Her resume was impressive; didn't you see that she worked at several Fortune 500 companies?"

By this point, I had become so angry that, in spite of knowing I might lose my job because my boss was kicking me under the table, I started in: "So let me get this straight. For a position that requires an individual to run an organization with offices across Canada, have fifteen people reporting directly to her, and handle over a hundred million dollars in budgets as well as over eight hundred employees, the only thing you did to verify her credentials was an interview and an in-basket test?"

I don't know if it was the way I stated it or whether they simply realized what they had done, but the owner began by saying how sorry they were that things had gone south and that they would help us find another person to fill her position.

At that point I looked over at my boss and said, "I'm going to give you my opinion, but what you choose to do with it is your business." Looking back at the recruiter, I said, "I think that you either return to us the fee you charged, minus administrative charges, or if we feel comfortable enough using your services again, you do not charge us for conducting another search and prove to us that you have done an extensive interview, a battery of tests [and I listed a bunch], *and* show us that you've hired an external firm to conduct extensive background checks."

I looked over at my boss, and he chimed in, "I agree with what she says."

King of the Jungle

I countered my boss, the Canadian sales manager, on an issue that I thought lacked reason. He came three inches away from my face (luckily the Scope kicked in), pointed at himself, and said, "I'm a Leo (as in astrologically). That means I'm *king* of this jungle . . . don't forget that." The fact that that was a verbal threat didn't affect me too much as I was so howling in laughter inside. What the heck did astrological signs have to do with the business issue at hand?

My first thought was to say, "I don't believe in astrology," but I didn't, as that may have been a career-limiting move. (You think?)

What I didn't see, and should have, was that this wasn't the place for me. It took me another year and a half to leave. The clues were all around.

It's All in the Details

We were in the process of coordinating a massive layoff of about two-thirds of the staff. I had spent weeks reviewing all of the employee files and working with an outplacement firm so that the layoffs could be handled as smoothly as possible. Part of the planning involved speaking with each senior executive and confirming which employees they needed to stay behind until we could close down the operations for good. The most important executive was the vice president of information technology. I had asked him on several occasions to hand me the list of which employees would be leaving us and which would be staying, and to confirm what the message should be to those employees who were being let go. About one week before the layoffs, I still had not heard back from him. So I got my boss to put some heat on him.

Finally, we got the list of employees. I went into his office to review the document with him, and he was very quick to brush me off. I kept reminding him that these people's livelihoods were at stake here, as well as the reputation of the company.

"Yes," he said. "I've done this multiple times and I know what I'm doing."

I left his office with a sinking feeling in my stomach. Sure enough, the day of the layoffs arrived. He was slated to speak to his group and personally deliver the message. We had taxis on standby to drive people home (if needed), as well as outplacement folks ready to speak with each employee. The VP started out by saying how sorry he was that people would be leaving. He then proceeded to talk, however, about what the company would be doing in moving forward and how exciting all of the changes were. The head of the outplacement firm was standing beside me and giving me the *look*, and I could hardly believe what I was hearing. After coaching him and guiding him, he was spewing off and no one was listening. After his spiel, I told the employees that outplacement people were there to help and the VP of the outplacement firm took over. As the employees made their way out of the room, two of them came over to the VP of IT and me. They looked at each other, smiling, and then said, "We have the codes for the servers and just wondered if you needed them before we leave."

Where's Waldo?

I once worked as a waitress for a large restaurant chain. We had recently hired a new manager for our location, and he seemed pretty nice. On one particularly busy evening, I needed his help with something and went to look for him. I couldn't find him. I walked everywhere through the restaurant, but everyone I asked could only tell me, "He was just here." It was like a bad game of *Where's Waldo?* After a few weeks of working with him I realized that, once the service got busy, he was nowhere to be found, and other waiters and waitresses complained about the same thing. About a month later, we found out he had been fired. Lo and behold, they had caught him hiding. It turns out he had found a cubby high above the restaurant with access through the kitchen. He used to hide there for the duration of the busy service time!

Taking Credit

I once worked with a boss who was about one year away from retirement. He was paranoid about keeping his job and was ruthless about taking credit for work from others and protecting himself at all costs.

One day, he walked into my office and asked if I could help him draft a policy. I jumped on the opportunity because it was going to be presented to the big brass during their monthly meetings. After working on it for almost a week straight and getting verification from my personal connections on two continents, I had what I thought was a well-drafted policy. Obviously, he thought so too, because two days later, I read an e-mail stating how he had drafted this new policy. Sure enough, when I opened up the attachment, it was the policy I had worked on.

Fast-forward a few months later, and my boss asked me to draft another policy, this time even larger in scope. I agreed but thought, *I'm only getting burned once.* Before I sent it to him, I e-mailed it to peers across the company asking them to review it and provide their feedback. After I hit *send*, I counted the seconds on one hand before I heard him coming down the hallway. He barged into my office, his face red and flushed, and asked me why I had sent the policy to the others. I looked at him calmly and, with a smile on my face, asked, "Didn't you ask us to work collaboratively at the last managers' meeting? I thought this would be a great opportunity to do just that." I knew he wanted to say more, or just strangle me, but he thought better of it and stormed out of my office.

A Quick Retort

I remember being interviewed for an HR manager's position at a very large firm. The person interviewing me was the supervisor to whom I would report, and we got along really well for the duration of the interview. Out of the blue, however, he asked me when I was going to get married and have children. It was one of those moments when you think to yourself, *I wish I had a quick comeback* and then, voilà, it came to me.

I looked him straight in the eye and said, "Oh, I see. You're testing me to see if I know what kinds of questions you can and cannot ask during an interview."

He took a few moments and realized I was giving him an out, which he took. After the interview, I was so proud of myself for actually coming up with a quick retort on the spot, as opposed to thinking of a good one during the drive home!

At the Casino

I worked with a supervisor in our plant who was so nervous about managing his team that he rarely showed up—only appearing at the end of the shift. Once when he was on vacation, his whole team decided to take off to a local casino. It was only when one of the supervisors in another part of the plant came over to check on his team that they realized they were gone. Did I mention that this was a team that was responsible for radiation units in the plant? Our supervisor was never reprimanded for that incident.

Payback

Okay, so picture this: I was corporate counsel, eight months pregnant, and working on this big deal to land a contract with a municipality. We had been slaving over this contract for most of my pregnancy. We were told that we were out of the running because we had not complied with the parameters of the bidding process. But we knew that we were in line with the regulations because we had submitted two bids—one that was compliant and the other that we knew wasn't but that had a better price on it.

I told my boss that, once we got kicked out, we would need to file an injunction to stop the procurement process from going forward. We had to prevent them from declaring another winner because they hadn't followed proper procedures in going through the bid process. The problem with going through an injunction was that time mattered. You only had x number of days to file the thing in order to stop the process and force them to do something else.

My boss had a strong type A personality and was very controlling. He had to be involved in the whole process. But I had decided (actually, the VPs and I had decided) that we didn't have time for him to review all the documents to confirm whether there was everything in them that he wanted to see. One day, I was sitting with the other VPs involved—as well as two other outside counsels—and we were on a conference call with my boss. I was explaining the whole procedure to him—what we had done, what we needed to do, and where we were going to go—and he said, "Okay, but you need to send it down to me so I can review and approve it before it goes out." The problem is, it needed to go out the next morning.

I said, "Great, Jim, but will you have it done by x time, because we need to issue it tomorrow morning, and we don't have time for you to review and approve it and start changing things. You just basically need to put your royal stamp on it and then we can send it out."

He replied, "This is what you need to do. I'm your boss and you listen to me."

There I was with two outside lawyers and two or three VPs, with me being eight months pregnant—but the rebuke didn't stop there. So I said, "Fine, Jim, we will do it your way. You can review it."

He proceeded to tear me a new one in front of my peers and coworkers. He asked how I dared "usurp his authority" and went on to say that he was the head of the project, that I couldn't tell him what to do, and "this is the process and there are no ifs, ands, or buts about it."

I was holding my tears in. After the whole thing was done, everyone in the room got really silent, and one of them asked me if I was okay. All I said was, "Yup."

So we went through and did what we needed to do. I don't think he ended up getting back to us in the time we needed to have it reviewed and approved, but we had already confirmed among ourselves that—whether he consented to it or not—it was going out as it was, because we had already done all of our work. So it went out and I think I spent the next day at home. He called me and said, "I need to talk to you about the phone call we had yesterday."

I said, "Jim, you had no right to do what you did. You were totally out of line. You tore me a new one on a conference call in front of my peers and external lawyers, and you made me look like an idiot."

He proceeded to say, "Yes, but you usurped my authority," but I cut the conversation short.

The next day he called again and we had a similar conversation, in which he reamed me out again for questioning his authority—or whatever. It got to the point where I said, "You know what? We are done with this conversation. I don't want to talk about it anymore." I continued, "Jim, I am pregnant, I am about to drop, and I have done nothing but focus on this baby (the project) instead of *my* baby. So enough is enough." Well, within a short period, I had the baby. Afterward, I think he came up to tell me something or to give me a review or something, and he said, "You know what? I owe you an apology."

"Oh?" I asked. "What for?"

He said, "For tearing a strip off of you and giving you a new one."

And I said, "Okay. Why did you do it?"

It turned out *his* boss had done exactly the same thing to him—torn a strip off him. And he ultimately realized that, despite the reason he had done it, it was wrong. "You were right," he said. "I should have never said those things to you." So it came around full circle and he realized that he had been a real *P*&^#*.

You Don't Understand Us

A good friend of mine had decided to transition into career counseling. Having been an HR professional for years, she thought she had very transferable skills. After working with a career counselor at a local counseling firm, an internal position became available and she was encouraged to apply for it. After successfully passing a forty-minute telephone prescreen she was invited in for an interview. To say she was excited was an understatement; the firm was a five-minute drive from her home and would offer comparable compensation to her past roles in HR.

When she arrived for the interview, she was told that they were running about a half hour late and was asked if she would she mind waiting. "Not at all," she said, and took a seat in the lobby. After forty minutes, the hiring manager walked out with a candidate and introduced herself; the manager said they needed about ten minutes to debrief on the previous candidates. So she sat back down and waited. Fifteen minutes later, the hiring manager returned.

By this time my friend had gone to get a drink of water. When the hiring manager saw the water bottle, she laughed and said, "We had water for you—you should have waited."

As she entered the boardroom, there were three people sitting around the table. She was a bit surprised, as this hadn't been mentioned. Things were progressing smoothly until they got to the last portion of the interview. The hiring manager said she didn't know if she was speaking on behalf of the others in the group, but said that she didn't know if this was going to be a good fit—and didn't know if they would have time to train my friend. She then went on to say that her secret desire had always been to employ someone from an HR background so that they could gain an appreciation of what they do, and that it would take years of practice to fully understand the complexity of what they did.

The manager then said that they would make their decision in the next week and that she would get a call informing her if she had made it to the final round of interviews. When she walked my friend to the lobby, she looked at her smiling and said, "Hey if things don't work out, you can always use our services. Have a great day!"

We Value You

Every year, the company I worked for would hold anniversary celebrations for those employees who had been with the organization for five years on up. On this occasion, one of my fellow coworkers who worked continental shifts was due to receive a special gift for reaching his fifteen-year anniversary. He was very excited about reaching this milestone and talked about it all week before the event. He attended the event, and the president of the company not only said wonderful things about him in front of his peers and management, but also presented him with a very nice, expensive gift. Imagine his shock the next day when he walked in and was told that he was being written up and would be given a day's suspension for not showing up for his shift the night before!

There's an enormous number of managers who have retired on the job.
—Peter Drucker

Sandbox Treasures

1. If the job forces you to hide, perhaps it is not the right one for you. Eventually, your staff or management will find you.
2. You can only take credit for other people's work once—or twice, if they aren't paying attention. Learn to do it on your own.
3. There is training and there are comedy routines; don't get them mixed up.
4. If spelling or any other skill is a company requirement, then everyone at the company should have it.
5. Karma . . . it's a beautiful thing!

SANDBOX PLAYMATES

They say that you spend more time working with others on the job than you do with your own family. Let's hope that you are in a situation where you get to spend it with people who make you laugh, especially at shared antics! I think my most memorable times at work were with people who shared my particularly weird sense of humor! Then, there are those coworkers who make you scratch your head and wonder, *What were they thinking?*

Just remember that you are not alone. For every weird or funny thing you have happen at work, there are other events—like those mentioned in the stories that follow—that may be even funnier or weirder!

It's a Good Idea, Right?

One of our bosses demanded we do an experiment for XYZ Company. They wanted some research data as soon as possible on some water filtration products. I volunteered with one of my coworkers, and we were sent home to grab an hour or so of sleep.

So it was three in the morning and we were getting tired, as we had to wait to refill water in tubs. (Just to give you an idea, these tubs were about fifteen feet high and about eight feet wide.) It was taking forever because we were using garden hoses to fill them up. Out of the corner of my eye, I spotted . . . a fire hose! I said to my coworker, "Hey, we can fill this thing in minutes if we use the fire hose."

"Great idea," he replied.

"Yeah, it makes sense. I'll unroll the hose and put it into the tub to fill it. You go and crank the water."

"Great, let's do it!" he responded.

He then cranked the water, but it wasn't just water. There was oil mixed with it. Water and oil went everywhere. Then it occurred to me: *Oh my God, we just triggered the fire alarm. Oh no, the cops and firemen are going to show up soon. Holy crap!* My coworker looked at me and said, "It's not such a good idea after all, eh?"

"You tell me that *now*?" was my reply.

We stayed for the rest of our shift, as nervous as could be. What if the cops showed up? What about the beer we'd had? What would we do about the mess? Finally, it was time to go home.

Once I got home, my wife asked how the night went. "Oh, fine," was my reply. When I woke up the next day, I asked her, "Did anyone from work call? Did anyone show up or stop by?" I got to work the next day and found out that, luckily, the fire alarm had been disconnected due to nonpayment or something!

Halloween

One Halloween, I dressed up like Madonna on her Blonde Ambition tour. I went the whole nine yards: I got a long, blonde wig and black fishnet stockings, and wore a brassiere made from orange safety cones, with gold tassels hanging from them. Apparently, however, I hadn't thought this through enough. I had sewn the cones into the bodysuit the night before and now had to drive into work. With those cones on, trying to steer the wheel was impossible, so I had to walk to the office. But the looks on my coworkers' faces when I showed up were priceless.

Cut and Paste

I had a project to complete, so I handed the material to a member of my staff and asked her to cut and paste several sections of the document using MS Word software. She was asked if she understood what was expected of her and she said, "Yes." So the material was left with her to finish.

The next day, I asked her if the task was done. In response, I was handed a document with all these typed labels taped onto the paper. I asked her, "What is this?"

She replied, "You asked me to cut and paste these sections using the word-processing software." I looked at her incredulously. She had told me she knew how to cut and paste, yet what she had done was literally *cut and paste* the sections onto the report using tape!

Welcome Home

I worked as a real estate agent for many years before I switched to a new career in building management. There were so many funny and weird situations I encountered during that time; here are but a few. I remember going to see a home before it was officially listed and the open house was scheduled. Imagine my surprise when I walked into the bedroom only to find two other real estate agents being intimate. In another situation, I had vendors that asked a lot of weird questions—or at least that I thought were weird. What direction does the sun come up on the house? Which part of the house is shady, and at what time of the day? They also spent a long time in the basement looking at the wiring, heating, and ventilation. I later found out they wanted to buy it in order to build a grow-op. At another time, I was showing a young couple through a house. It's not unusual for people to open closets, doors, and so forth as they make their way around the house. As we reached the bedroom, I decided to open up the huge double doors of their closet. To my horror, a *very large, unusual,* and apparently very well-used "toy" dropped from the top shelf onto the floor and rolled to my feet. I looked over at the couple to see if they had seen it, and sure enough—judging by the looks on their faces—they had. My dilemma was then *how do I put the thing back?* I didn't want to leave it out. So I ran into the bathroom, grabbed a towel, picked *it* up, and put it back on the top shelf. Later, I had an opportunity to meet the owners of the house while finalizing the terms of the offer. Talk about an awkward situation, because they neither looked nor acted like a couple that would be into that kind of thing.

That's Not Funny

How's this for impressing your new coworkers? I worked for a multinational chain as a corporate operations trainer. On the second day of on-the-job training, my estranged boyfriend walked into the lobby and announced that, if I didn't come out and talk to him, he would blow the place up! Wearing a rather thick jacket that made it look like he had bombs attached to his body, he sat on the curb of the head office, crying and yelling that I was the love of his life. I later found out he had done this as a ploy to win me back; he hadn't had any bombs on him or any intention of harming anyone, and he thought it was rather amusing. He did it for attention. For weeks afterward, I was constantly teased about the episode.

Voice Mail

I worked for one of the top staffing agencies in San Francisco. One of my coworkers was called "the person in charge of the Freak Desk," because the calls she got from our temp employees calling in their availability were out of this world. This is just a sample:

"Hey. I'm calling in with my availability, and if I was standing out on the pier waving a white hankie at all the sailors, I could not be more available."

"I am calling in available, willing to do anything including shoveling shit, but nothing with barnyard animals."

Vanilla

I once worked for a firm with four others in a cubicle area. We had recently hired another person, and it wasn't too long before all of us noticed that, after eating, he would pass a lot of gas. It got to the point where none of us wanted to be in the same room with him when he got back from lunch. So, of course, all of my coworkers ganged up on me and "elected" me to go and talk with him. I agonized about it all day, but finally thought of an idea that might make it a bit easier to handle.

So I asked him (before lunch, LOL!) to talk to me in the lunchroom. I started off the conversation by saying that sometimes, different kinds of foods react differently with different people. I told him that I used Beano if I knew I was going to have something that gives me gas. He was nodding at me the whole time and then he thanked me profusely for coming to talk to him about the issue. Well, I guess he thought an external solution was better than an internal one, because the next day he started spraying vanilla-scented room freshener every time he passed gas. So not only did we know for sure when he was going to fart, the smell was ten times more awful, because it was mixed with some cheap vanilla-scented spray. To this day, I cannot stand the scent of vanilla!

Gotcha!

We used to have water games at one company I worked for. On Friday afternoons, everybody would be tired and in need of a break. So at three o'clock, everybody would start loading up water guns. We would shoot at each other in the hallways and in the tower. People would get garbage bags on to protect themselves so they wouldn't get wet, and they would even come out of the elevators. It was like kamikaze-type stuff, with all of us trying to get each other!

Did That Just Happen?

I was interviewing someone for a position in our materials department. It was a Friday afternoon around four fifteen. Our conversation seemed to flow, so this was an easy interview. He was asking as many questions as I was and I was enjoying the interaction. He seemed to be a good fit for the position and the organization, and I was looking forward to introducing him to our materials manager.

The interview was beginning to wind down when a person in a senior management position suddenly opened the door to my office, poked his head inside, and said:

"I've had enough of this place! I'm getting the f-ck out of here!" Then he closed the door—and left!

I tried to wipe that "I can't believe that just happened!" look off my face and apologized to the gentleman across the table. He gave a nervous chuckle and appeared to brush it off. We concluded the interview without any mention of the incident.

I Know

I worked with someone who eventually became a good friend. During the early months of us working together, she admitted during our lunch hour (which we would spend outdoors when we could) that she was secretly smoking behind her husband's back. Every lunch hour she would puff on her smokes and then put them in the back trunk of her car, because her husband *never* looked there. Imagine the look on our faces when, one day, she opened up her trunk to find a note attached to her hidden smokes: "I know. Love, your husband."

Wedgie

The accounting supervisor, the general manager, and I were in the archive room at work when our then–vice president of operations walked into the room. The accounting supervisor was bent over, going through a box, so the VP reached down her trousers, pulled her undies up, said, "Got ya! Wedgie pull!" and then walked out in hysterics! Needless to say, a few more instances of the same nature caused him to be the ex-VP!

Dolls at Work

I once worked for an insurance company that had a really funny HR manager working there. She always had quotations on her office door and really did her best to encourage and mentor others at the company. The company was going through some major changes: some good, some not so much. The tension in the office was brutal at times. I remember that, when she came back from visiting our offices in the United States, she brought back one of those Weebles blow-up punching dolls. It looked like a fighter, and when you hit it, it would say, "Come on! Is that all you've got?" It was a great stress reliever for everyone, and it got us all laughing—especially during those awful months of change.

Leave a Message

I once worked with someone who always answered the phone with a fake phone message. She would make the sound of the beep (which she had down pat) and then proceed to say, "Hi, you have reached ____. I'm not here right now, but please leave a message at the tone." As soon as the person on the other end would start to talk, she would yell out, "I'm here!" She would always laugh and tell us it sounded like the person had dropped the phone!

Making an Entrance

A coworker and I were in Arizona and I had to give a huge speech at the Mesa Convention Center. There were several thousand people there. I gave a wonderful talk and the host organization was going to honor us. They were going to give us an award and a dinner on a special cruise ship on a lake near the Superstition Mountains.

Before we made our way to the lake, however, I told my business partner I wanted to freshen up. "Let's run back to our hotel room and get changed," I said. "I feel kinda grungy." So we went back into town and drove as fast as we could to our hotel. The event organizers were worried that we were going to be late, but we said we would be back in time.

So we were racing back and we got lost on the Apache Indian Reservation. We were driving a brand new Lexus and swerving in and out of the cacti, and this old Native American came up to us on a burro. We tried to ask him for directions to where we had to go, and he pointed us toward a small town up in the mountains called Apache Junction. Eventually, we got to an old saloon and there were all these old prospectors in there, with chaps and guns; we felt as though we were in the Old West. There were spittoons on the floor and we could literally hear the pinging when the men spat in them.

We walked into the saloon with our suits, feeling a little out of place, and we asked the woman behind the bar where the lake was. She gave us directions and off we went! We had to whip along this old country road with a barrier alongside it. We were going so fast that my business partner was pulling chunks out of his seat! We finally got there, and just as we pulled into the marina, we saw the ferry pull out. It was like one of those old paddleboats you see in Louisiana.

The ferry was way out there. So I looked at this guy who had just brought his motorboat into the marina and asked him, "For ten bucks, will you take us out there?" He agreed. I gave him the ten bucks and he whipped us out toward the ferry. Just as we were approaching the cruise ship, I poised myself on the bow of our little boat. Everyone from the cruise ship was cheering us on as we stepped across and onto the deck of the bigger vessel. We walked through a crowd of people who were clapping, patting us on the back, and laughing and whistling at us, and the organizer looked over at us and said, "Now *that* was an entrance!"

Right Place, Right Time

One summer, I worked as a security guard for a bakery. Located across the street were some hotels and motels that catered to *hourly clientele*, shall we say. On one particular Sunday afternoon, my coworker decided that, rather than taking his rounds through the plant, he would walk around the outside, along the perimeter. As he stepped out of the front door, he heard a woman screaming from across the street. She was being beaten up by some guy. So my coworker ran across the road, while radioing the other guards he worked with to call 911.

He started yelling at the guy to leave her alone when, out of the corner of his eye, he saw this car pull up with New York license plates. It ran up over the curb, came to a screeching halt in front of the woman and man, and out jumped this guy who was massive. The newcomer pulled the man off of her, slammed him into the ground, and put him into this weird position that basically immobilized him. When the police arrived, one of them said to the guy, "That was pretty impressive how you got him down so quickly. Can I ask what you do for a living?"

The guy responded, "I'm a marine, and I'm on leave."

Reply All

I run my own IT company and one of my employees sent an e-mail to me indicating that he wasn't sure things were being run the way they should be. Some of his points represented fair feedback to give to your boss. The only problem was that he sent it *reply all*, so everyone at the company read his note. I approached him and asked him whether it had been his intention to send the e-mail to everyone. Judging by his reaction, he was mortified by what he had done, so I didn't fire him.

When I retired from the company, a party was thrown for me. During the party, that employee stood up and talked about my character and how, in his mind, he should have been fired for that mistake, but that my response had won him undying respect for me.

Al, Is That You?

I worked at a library system way, way back, and the commands were two-letter commands. One day we had a meeting reminder, but back then—in the days well before the invention of the Microsoft Suite—such reminders came as alarm notices. They would pop up reading *AL*, and then the notice would describe what the alarm was for. One of our clients called later that day and said, "How did you know my name was Al?" I had to explain to him that everyone got the same alarm notice that always started with AL.

Can I Have Your Cart?

I once worked as a manager covering for a maternity leave with a local big-box home renovation store. The store had several employees who had retired but still worked in various departments. They were experts in their field, had really great customer service skills, and were willing to mentor and coach some of the younger staff. They also tended to move a bit more slowly, and I didn't realize how much so until this one incident. On this one occasion I asked Bob, who worked in the paint department, if I could take the cart up to the front of the store for him, as he was pushing it in that direction. Bob looked up, smiled, and said, "Nope, I need it to walk."

I Know Where You Sit

In my very first job out of university, I had the cubicle right outside the women's bathroom. I'm sure you can picture that every woman in the company knew who I was, because they had to walk past me to get to the toilet. And I could almost predict "situations" by the amount of time they would spend in the washroom. I remember being in one particular meeting. When it came time to introduce ourselves, one of the ladies piped up: "I know you. You're the guy who sits outside of the women's bathroom!" Talk about being mortified!

Fire!

I was working as an assistant manager for a large cinema complex for about three months before I was transferred to their large eight-hundred-seat theater downtown. My first night there I was told that I would be in charge of handling the opening of *Dragonheart* and that all of the top executives would be in attendance. To say that I was nervous was an understatement, but I gathered all of my staff and reviewed our procedures to ensure that everyone was prepared. Part of the preparation was splicing the movie; back then it wasn't digital as it is today.

We finished our preparations, the movie began, and for the first five minutes everything ran smoothly. I decided, at that time, to step out into the lobby and ensure that the rest of the staff was okay. Suddenly one of my staff came running toward me with a look of panic on his face. He reached me, face flushed, and told me, "Sir, sir your screen is burning up!" I asked him, "What do you mean?" He answered that the screen was on fire—that it was burning up.

I start running toward the theater, my heart nearly beating out of my chest as I envisioned the theater bursting into flames and the ensuing mayhem. I thought, *This can't be happening*, as I pushed the theater doors open. I looked up and to my relief realized that the theater was *not* on fire; the film had caught in the machine and was burning—and *that's* what was being projected onto the screen!

I rushed up to the projector room, only to find film everywhere! I turned to the projectionist and asked him, "Why didn't you call me?" He replied, "My radio died." So I worked furiously with him to try to get the film fixed. Once that was under control, I walked back downstairs and announced what the problem was and how we were working to fix it. I then informed everyone that they would be receiving free passes to make up for the delays while we repaired the damage.

As I walked off the stage, all I could think was, *I'm going to be fired for this fiasco.* As it turned out, they all thought I did a great job of handling the situation, and I was ultimately promoted to the manager's position. I did end up talking to my staff and reviewing fire safety!

There are two kinds of people: those who do the work and those who take the credit. Try to be in the first group; there is less competition there.
—Indira Gandhi

Sandbox Treasures

1. Lack of sleep and great ideas don't mix.
2. Voice mail *is* a permanent record.
3. You only get one chance to make a memorable entrance, so grab it when you can!
4. Sometimes you have to give the benefit of the doubt to an employee.
5. Being at the right place at the right time can make a huge difference.

SANDBOX VISITORS

It doesn't matter what field you're in; chances are you have to deal with clients or customers in one way or another. My grandmother laughed when I told her that I got a job as a waitress. Asking her what was so funny, she smiled and said, "There is nothing like working with the public." She was so right!

I now think that getting a job and working with the public—in either a paid or volunteer capacity—should be a high school prerequisite. There is no better education, in my mind, than having to deal with some of the weird and funny situations that occur when you work with others. It teaches you patience, understanding, and resourcefulness.

Clams

I worked as a waitress in a seafood restaurant. One day, I approached a table with a couple and a small child to take their order. I finished taking the order from the mother and father, and then the mother and I turned to the small boy and asked him what he would like for dinner. "Well," he said, looking at his parents, "I'm not sure. But I think I would like to order clams." I looked at him, smiling, and asked, "*Clams*? Are you sure you want to eat clams?"

"Well, my dad eats clams all the time," he said, "and I heard my mom say that Dad eats her clam all the time." Needless to say, there was a moment of silence, and then the whole section erupted in laughter.

What Are You Doing?

I had a client who was having his lunch at the park. A woman drove into the nearby lot and parked her car. My client described her as being *tartly dressed*, whatever that meant. He saw her get out of her car and into a Cadillac that was parked a few spaces down. My client then saw the woman's head disappear from view. After a few minutes, he saw the lady exit the Cadillac, get back into her own car, and drive away. My client decided that this looked pretty interesting and that he would like to meet this lady. So he followed her back to work.

The lady later said that she sensed someone was following her. So she eventually stopped her car and confronted my client. She thought that he had been hired as a private investigator by her husband to spy on her, to see if she was having an affair. My client didn't try to dissuade her from this notion. Instead, he played along and said he was going to share the information about her and the guy in the Cadillac. My client said, "Why don't we get together and have lunch ourselves in the park?"

The lady responded, "Yeah, that would be a good idea. Why don't we meet at the Holiday Inn?"

"No, I couldn't meet at a hotel after work," my client replied. "I'm married and I have to get home to my wife."

"Okay, so why don't we meet at the park?"

"Great idea," he agreed.

So off he went to the park the next day, but—for some reason—the cops had an undercover officer stationed there. My client pulled in and then the lady did too. As she got out of her car, my client drove up to her. She got into his car to see what he wanted to do, and then the cops arrested him for soliciting sex.

Believe it or not, his arrest is still not the most interesting part of the story, because the case went to trial. At the trial, the lady sat in the witness box looking like she was a schoolteacher. She had a white, frilly blouse on, and my client barely recognized her. That certainly wasn't the way she had dressed that day! (My client had said she was dressed like a streetwalker.)

At cross-examination time, I got the chance to ask her questions, and I thought, *I am going to find out what's going on here.* I knew that all of the players were married—she was married, my client was married, and so was the guy in the Cadillac—so nobody wanted to share anything. So I asked her, "What was your purpose in going to the park that day?" and she replied that she was meeting a friend. "How well do you know this friend?" I continued, and she answered that they had met online. "Well, did you go there with the purpose of having sex with him?" I persisted, and she said that, no, she hadn't. "So what were you doing in the car then, since your head was not visible?"

"Merely performing fellatio," she answered.

"Okay. So in your mind," I continued, "merely performing fellatio is not considered sex?"

"Yes," she replied.

Character Reference

I have retyped (verbatim), a letter of character reference that was included in a candidate's application package with the board. I have omitted the name of the referee and have renamed the candidate "Sara" for confidentiality reasons.

In my opinion, the content of the letter is inappropriate and should not have been included with the application package—or *any* employment application package for that matter!

Although "personal" or "character" references are inadmissible, I did caution "Sara" about the lack of propriety of the letter she had provided as part of her package. However, much to my surprise and disappointment, she was neither embarrassed nor apologetic and left me with the impression that I had overreacted. I'll let you be the judge . . .

> *To whom it may concern,*
>
> *I have known Sara for over five years now initially as a work colleague, from that time progressing into personal friendship.*
>
> *Through seeing her at work and on a social level (and boy is she sociable!) I would consider her to be an upstanding, when sober which I have to concede is not often, trustworthy, if you don't leave temptation in the way, wallets . . . handbags, etc., individual for whom I would always readily stand reference. After all I've stood bail often enough!*
>
> *Since meeting her spouse, is it no. 2, 3?? You lose count don't you? Sara has stopped sleeping around which is a relief, as I, as a nurse, firmly believe you can take so much penicillin, it can't cure every strange infection all the time.*

Her move to Canada will result in many tears from her friends and family, as she owes all of them money, I have warned her that crack cocaine is addictive. However she does insist she will pay all the money back, as she told me that prostitution is very lucrative in Canada as the locals are not as fussy as the English!

With regards,

It Is a Sales Position

My father owns his own sales company. He was approached by a government-sponsored employee referral program that was going to present him with prescreened candidates for a sales position. So he agreed to participate in the program.

The first candidate who was presented to him had notes attached to her file (her background, her resume, and so forth). On the last page, it stated that she could not be employed by any company where she might run the risk of being fired. "Why on earth would they send me someone like this?" my father asked me. "It's a sales position," he continued. "Of course there's a strong possibility of her being fired if she doesn't meet her sales quotas!"

Who's First?

For my first summer job I worked in an amusement park that had a go-kart track. It was situated in a very rough part of town, but the people I worked with were an absolute blast. One night we had a particularly rough crowd, and a very inebriated individual started harassing me and got pretty aggressive when I told him he could not ride the go-karts because of his physical state. When my fellow coworkers backed me up, he came within two inches of my face and said, "Fine, I'll just be waiting for you after work." I often got remarks like this, but there was something different in this guy's tone that made me think twice about leaving work on my bike as usual. So when I was on my break, I called my dad to come and pick me up.

Sure enough when my shift was finished, I saw the guy waiting for me. I got into the car, and the guy approached my dad along with a couple of his friends. Then he started in on how he was going to get both my dad and me.

Now picture this: my dad is about six feet two and weighed about 240 pounds at that time. The three guys were all really skinny, and the one leader who had threatened me was wearing a T-shirt with *I am the buzzard and I am stoned* on it.

Without missing a beat, my father calmly took his cigar out of his mouth, dropped it on the ground, and ground it with his foot—all the while watching the boys. He then took off his jacket and casually tossed it up in the tree; it landed on one of the branches. He started rolling up his sleeves and turned to them saying, "Okay, boys. One a time." The whole thing looked so beautifully choreographed that the boys freaked and ran off.

In the car on the drive home, my dad and I were cracking up. I told him, there is no way he could *ever* repeat that throw-your-jacket-on-a-tree-limb routine again!

How Would You Handle It?

I work as a manager for a large retail chain, and we had this customer who wanted to purchase a scarf, but there was no price on it. So she went up to one of the associates who worked at the store and asked how much the scarf was. The associate went to the rack with all of the other scarves and then quoted her $19.99, based on some other scarves that were comparable in make and quality. The customer replied, "Excuse me, where did you come up with that number?"

So the associate said, "I work here every day and know the price of the items. The scarf you have is comparable to others we have priced at $19.99."

The customer replied by saying, "I want to speak with a manager."

Now, normally, we like our associates to deal directly with the customers to try to learn how to handle difficult people, but since she was loud and very rude, I decided to step in to help. So I went over and asked, "How can I help you?"

"This gentleman just made up the price of this scarf," she stated.

I told her I would go look to confirm the scarf's correct price, although he had already looked and it was most likely the right price. I took a peek at her scarf and saw that it was a Ralph Lauren and that it was priced at $39.99. So I let her know this fact but told her that I would let her have it for $19.99. "That is not the price!" she screamed at me. "What are people doing around here—just making up the prices as they go along, or based on how they feel for the day? How is this company still in business? You should change the company manual!"

I explained to her that, even though there wasn't an exact match for her scarf with a price on it, usually the same make is priced at the same price point. "We don't make prices based on our *feelings*. We make them based on the product," I said. "Look," I continued, "at $19.99, you're getting a good deal on a scarf that typically sells for $39.99."

"I told you!" she yelled back. "It's not about the price! It's about you guys making the prices up and that's a rip-off."

This was such a strange situation. I could only think to make an argument based on a business case. So I asked her, "How would you handle it, then, if I were you and you were me? How would you get the price?"

And she said, "*Excuse me?* What do you mean, how would *I* get the price?"

"Well, how would you get the price if you didn't have the exact same item?"

"How *dare* you ask me a question like that!" she yelled. "You are the worst manager I have ever come across."

"I didn't mean to offend you," I replied. "Listen. I just want to give you the scarf at the best price."

"Worst management I have ever seen!" she yelled before storming off—and buying the scarf at our downstairs checkout desk.

Now Be Nice

I work in a retail environment, and one day we had a customer complain about the service she was being given by one of my coworkers. The client said, "She is so unbelievably slow and generally very rude."

"Ma'am," I said, "I'm going to be straight with you. If you are going to say bad things about the people who work here, I will not help you. If you are polite and kind, though, then I will do the best I can to help you." Her reply to this was, "I am *sooo* sorry."

Bath Time

Although I clean homes for a living, there are some situations where I take on more responsibility as favors to friends. One example is the time I took on the personal care of an older gentleman.

The first day I arrived at the home, I rang the doorbell several times. When he finally opened the door, he was standing there, *stark naked* and *erect!*

"Oh my God!" I said.

I gave him the up and down, and he said, "Hi. Nice to meet you."

I said, "Let's get you inside [as he had stepped outside to greet me] and get a robe on you." We both went upstairs and got ready for his bath. Once in the bath, he asked if I could wash a little lower. I said, "No. Remember our deal. You wash your personals, and I'll wash your body."

He replied, "Yes . . . but it feels so good!"

Please Don't Show Me

Working at the go-kart track was a blast. Getting to spend all day in the sun was great. (Okay, so back then it wasn't as harmful, or at least we were ignorant about the issue.) It was my first job, and I was so excited at the prospect of making $4.25 an hour. (Why is it that, as a kid, you make peanuts, but feel that you're making a ton of cash, yet by the time you're making great money, you don't feel like you have enough?)

We had so many different kinds of people coming to the go-kart track, and I think this was my first real dose of customer service. We had strict rules when it came to safety—like, if you had long hair, you had to pull it up under the helmet we provided. I had one kid argue with me that his hair wasn't quite long enough to get stuck in the go-kart and then, just to prove his point, he took off his helmet and started taking strands of his hair and trying to get them caught in the engine behind him!

Watch Them!

One summer I worked in a provincial park in northern Ontario. We typically got a lot of customers from all over the world who wanted to experience a typical Canadian summer—canoeing, fishing, and so on. More often than not, we had customers whose first language was not English, but we managed to provide them with safety rules and ensure that they understood the basics of how to manage a canoe. I still remember this couple that came in; they seemed to understand all of the rules and basic safety for canoeing, despite the language barrier. Once they stepped into the canoe, it became apparent that they hadn't understood at all. The man sat at the front of the canoe facing forward, while his wife sat at the back of the canoe facing the opposite direction from her husband. They started paddling and trying to get away from the dock. As you can imagine, paddling in opposite directions didn't get them anywhere! So the wife started yelling at her husband, waving her hands around—to which her husband replied by yelling back at her. They got louder and louder, and I was trying to explain what they were doing wrong, but they weren't even looking at me because they were so focused on yelling at each other. At that point, I looked up and saw another couple paddling by, and I got an idea. I wolf whistled, got their attention, and then pointed to the couple paddling by. They sat watching for a few moments and proceeded to paddle away from the dock successfully.

My Girls

I work as a manager for a large computer chain. Typically, we get a lot of customers coming in with various questions about computers not working, and so forth. Normally, I let the junior staff handle these situations and treat them as learning opportunities. This one day, however, I happened to be on the floor, serving customers, when one lady walked in and demanded to see the manager immediately.

When I walked over, I saw a woman who was very well-dressed, with obvious good taste in clothes. She was put together from head to foot. She barely let me get out, "How can I help you?" before she started frantically waving her phone in front of me and stating that it wasn't working and that she couldn't operate her business without it. She then proceeded to show me her "girls" on the phone. "See, isn't this girl pretty? And this one too?" she asked. "I need my phone to operate my business," she continued. "And, you see, if I cannot get calls, I cannot get my girls working." In all my years in this business, I can honestly say that this was the first time I was absolutely speechless!

Milk Police

I work in a deli in a major commercial center that houses quite a few large corporations. We used to get quite a few customers who made me really question their behavior. We had one gentleman who would appear at the counter every lunch hour like clockwork, try every version of a particular meat we sold, and make comments on each one. On Monday, for instance, he would try the ham: black forest—*too salty*, honey ham—*too sweet*, dry ham—*too dry*, sandwich ham—*too watery*, and so forth. After giving him all the samples, we would ask, "Are you going to buy any?"—to which he would look at us and say, "Oh, I am not going to get anything, at least not today!"

In another instance we had a lady who wanted to purchase some roast beef that we had on sale. The price per pound was marked on a sign with two prongs that stuck into the roast in the display case. She looked at the price and then said, "You have the roast on sale for $4.99/lb.?" "Yes," I replied. Then, without missing a beat, she asked how much it was for half a pound. I looked at her thinking she was teasing me or something, but she had a serious look on her face. So I replied, "Half of $4.99." "Oh, okay," she said and kept looking at the display case. As near as I can guess, she was really trying hard to figure out what that price was. I later found out that she was the comptroller for the large telecommunications firm down the road. That incident made me want to check out my phone bill when I got home that night!

We had a couple that used to come in every week and buy their milk together, which was a huge production. The milk we sold was the kind with three bags of milk contained in one large plastic bag. They would open up each of the plastic bags, check to see which individual bag of milk had more in it, and then they would put together their own three bags of milk. This whole production would take about a half hour and literally make a mess of the milk section because they weren't very careful about reassembly. After about three weeks of this, my manager came out and spoke with them, informing them that all of the milk was automatically measured out by machine and that what they were doing really wasn't productive; it was just making a mess, and they weren't getting any more milk in one bag versus another. The man tried to argue with my manager, but he really didn't get anywhere with him, so they walked off to purchase their milk.

The next week we saw the couple walking toward the milk section, and we alerted our manager, who headed them off at the pass. This time the conversation was a bit more heated, and we overheard the man telling our manager that he looked it up online and was convinced that it was not as automated as the manager had told him; he said that very often there was a difference of a few ounces of milk in each bag. The manager told him in no uncertain terms that he could either buy the milk *as is*, or he would be banned from the store because of the mess he kept leaving. So the couple left the store, without their milk.

The following week, I saw the couple walking around the store, carefully looking around for the manager and walking slowly toward the milk section. We again alerted our manager who then waited by our deli counter, adjacent to the milk section. As soon as he saw the man reach for the milk bag to open it, my manager walked up to him and grabbed the milk bag from him. The man was outraged and started screaming at the manager, telling him that it was his right to examine the milk bags and how dare he prevent him from doing so. Our manager was really good at calming him down, and then he had them both escorted out of the store. Later that week, we had our staff meeting in which we were told that the "milk couple" were now officially banned from the store—and if we were to spot them we were to call security. For several weeks after that meeting, we used the term *milk police* for anyone assigned the task of looking out for the couple!

Thirteen and Important

I work as an electrician for a large utilities company. One day, a coworker and I were at a site where there was a power outage: a line had come down in a residential survey. So I was out there in the truck, and we had to go all over the survey trying to get the power back on. All of a sudden, this girl came over to the truck—she was about thirteen years old—and she started yelling and screaming at us, saying, "They told us that the power was going to be on by this time, and it's not on! If it's not on soon, I'm going to throw my phone at you, because I need to charge it so I can text people!"

My coworker and I both started laughing at her, and she got even more upset. We said, "If you throw the phone at us, then you won't even *have* a phone!"

"You guys don't care because you can probably charge your phones in your truck!" she yelled, and then she walked away in a huff. I thought, *Who is so important that they can't wait for a text from a thirteen-year-old?*

Flowers and Lipstick

I worked for a company that delivered flowers to various large chains throughout Canada and the United States. Each day of the week, we had to call in for different orders and take incoming calls as well. On one particular day, I got a call from one of the large purchasers located down in Georgia. In a southern drawl, my contact started off by saying, "Hey, ____, you are never gonna believe this."

"Hi. How are you?" I replied. "And what's going on?"

"Well," she said, "your driver showed up, and he's wearin' women's lipstick, women's stockings, and women's high heels. We have a problem."

"Excuse me?" I said.

She said, "Yup. You heard me right, girl, and if he's headin' Mississippi way, they're gonna kill him up there. I'm tellin' ya, they will *kill* him."

"Hold on a second," I said, and I called for the transportation manager.

"What's going on?" he asked.

"Just tell me," I replied, "the driver we have in Georgia right now—is he heading to Mississippi? Apparently, he's dressed like a woman, and if he's on his way to Mississippi, they're gonna kill him down there."

"Well, yes," he answered, "he is on his way to Mississippi." So I got back on the phone with our contact and told her that he was, in fact, on his way to Mississippi.

"Well," she said, "you'd better tell him to clean his act up, 'cause they are gonna kill him otherwise."

"Okay," I responded. "Please don't call ahead to the stores and get them all excited. We'll take it from here, okay?"

"Okay. You take care of it, honey," she replied.

I swear it must have been about ten minutes later that I got a call from another store in Georgia, because they'd gotten a call from the original store in the area, alerting them that this driver was coming. The lady started in right away and said, "We are gonna be on the lookout for this driver, and if there is anythin' funny 'bout him, we are gonna send him away, okay?"

I reassured her that everything was going to be fine. "Please call me when he's finished with his delivery," I said.

"Okay. That's what we'll do."

So the driver made the delivery and everything turned out okay, as he had cleaned himself up. When the store called to confirm this, they said, "Well, he did have traces of women's lipstick on him, but other than that, he was fine." I had never come across anything like this on the job before—and I never have since!

I'm Protected

I worked for a ski resort as a ski instructor. One winter, I was training a fellow who had never skied before. Every time he fell, I kept hearing a *popping* sound. After about five or six tumbles and the ensuing pops, I just had to ask him what that sound was. He looked at me and, smiling, opened his jacket. He had wrapped himself in layers of bubble wrap!

I Am So Ready for This Job

After setting a temp up with a very high-profile position, reviewing what she was looking for and preparing her for success, she said, "I am so ready for this opportunity! I'll be there and I'll wow them!" Five minutes into the interview, my client called up and asked why I had sent this person to her. When I asked why, she responded that my applicant had flatly said she wasn't interested in this kind of work—all within the first two minutes of the interview!

Piss Off

I worked in a nursing home as a director. We had a patient who used to harass this one nursing assistant. He would follow her, yell at her, and just generally be a pest. One day, I guess she had finally had it with him. She turned to him and said, "Mr. ___, piss off." So he opened his bathrobe and started urinating on her!

A Dozen Doughnuts

I worked as a corporate operations trainer for a rather large doughnut chain. We were required to assist with hiring and training the staff on company procedures. I remember training this rather timid and shy girl on the front cash. After a couple of days, we felt she was ready to handle customers on her own. Her first customer asked for a dozen doughnuts, and without missing a beat, she smiled at him and asked, "Is that for here or to go?"

Twenty-Five Cents

All through university, I worked for a video store chain. Some customers would rack up rather large late charges. I remember this one customer telling me that, even though he had twenty-eight dollars in late charges, he wouldn't fail to return this next movie "on time." When I told him that I couldn't let him rent another movie without paying down his late charges, he reached into his pocket, handed me twenty-five cents, and asked, "Will this do?"

Thanks for Sharing

I was in my second week on the job with a major multinational firm and we had HR meetings in Orlando, Florida. I was asking our vice president of HR—who had been in HR for thirty years—what was the most interesting job interview he had ever carried out.

Apparently, he had been working for a bank in Atlanta, Georgia, and a candidate had come in. About halfway through the interview, my VP was thinking, *This guy is not going to cut it*—but he chose to finish the session off. At the end of the interview, my VP asked the candidate what I guess was a standard question: "Do you have any other skills or abilities that you think I should know about?"

The candidate looked at him and said, "Yes. I'm a former Green Beret, and I just want you to know that I could be across this desk and cutting your throat in a second and a half, and no one would ever hear me."

The VP looked at him, horrified, and was thinking, *How do I get this guy out of my office?* But the VP just looked at him and said, "Well, thank you so much for coming in. I will actually refer you to our security division, as they may have a need for someone with your unique abilities. We'll be in touch."

Uniform

I was working as a senior labor relations officer in a health-care facility when I got a call from the manager of our porters division. Now, the porters are the staff members who take patients to x-ray appointments, lab tests, and so forth. The manager of the department was pretty hot under the collar when he called me, demanding to see me right away. I thought it was odd, as I couldn't remember doing anything incorrectly for him. In fact, I couldn't even remember the last time we'd spoken.

I hustled over and he said he had a problem with the dispatch office. When I asked him what the issue was, he said, "I always tell my dispatch person to be ready fifteen minutes before their shift starts."

I said, "Okay."

He proceeded to say that Earl had showed up at 2:45 p.m. for his shift that started at 3:00 p.m., and again I asked, "Okay, but what is the issue?" He continued that Earl had walked into the dispatch office and caught the dispatcher, whom he was going to relieve, wearing nothing but his bra and panties. All I could say to this was, "Oh."

"Yes, Earl is a bit freaked out," he said. "We disciplined Bob, but his union local president indicated that Bob's defense was that he had *gender identification issues*—and that was why he wasn't wearing his uniform. I told the union president that I can understand that and that we work in a hospital, so we can get him assistance. I'm not disciplining him for the underwear he was wearing. I'm disciplining him for the uniform that he wasn't wearing! If he had been sitting there in his skivvies or boxers we would still be having the same conversation."

"Quite frankly," I said, "he doesn't see the public, so if he feels more comfortable wearing a female uniform, we can issue him one—but he has to wear it!"

I Don't Want to Shake Hands

I once participated in an interview where the candidate kept picking his nose throughout the entire interview. All I kept thinking about was, *Do I have to shake his hand at the end of the interview?* Aside from being totally disgusted, I was so distracted I barely finished the interview. I kept trying to think of reasons to not shake his hand at the end of the interview!

Mix-Up

I was working for a major photo-finisher in western Canada. The worst thing you can do in our business—from the point of view of a production employee—is a *mix*. A mix is where we send the customer the wrong negatives and the right prints, or vice versa.

I was working in our Edmonton office when I heard our production manager laughing hysterically in the next office. Curious, I walked over and asked what was going on. He said, "Well, we just had the mother of all mixes."

"Really? What happened?" I asked.

"Well," he said, "we had a couple of enlargements that we had to do. One was for an elderly lady here in the city, and the photos were of her granddaughter's wedding. It was a group shot of the wedding party. We also had a young lady who had some shots of her private region and she wanted an eight-by-ten of them." (What the young lady was going to do with these eight-by-tens I don't know, but we actually produce shots like that as long as they don't involve contact with other people, or porn.)

"Anyways," my manager continued, "we mixed them up and I am now trying to deal with the aftermath." He then looked at me and said, "I can only imagine what the grandmother thought of the picture when she opened up the envelope!"

Merry Christmas

In another story, at this same photo-finishing company, part of our business was producing photographic Christmas cards. During the holiday season, I was working in my colleague's office in Detroit when our production manager came in laughing and said, "Guys, check this out. We got an order for Christmas cards, and this gentleman wants two hundred copies of this card printed up."

He handed us the card. It was a picture of a gentleman (and I use the term loosely) wearing nothing but a Santa hat. It was a full-frontal nude, and the caption read, "Ho, ho, ho. Check this out! Merry Christmas!" Needless to say, my colleagues and I were debating to whom you would send such a card.

Wrestling

A large percentage of the job candidates I interview are teenagers looking for part-time employment on weekends and after school. Last week, I interviewed a young man. When querying his availability, I asked him whether or not he was involved in anything (such as a sports team) that would prevent him from being able to maintain his "open" availability. He proceeded to tell me that he had been seriously involved in wrestling, but that this wouldn't alter his availability since he wouldn't be wrestling this year. Curious, I asked him why he wasn't wrestling this year, as he seemed to enjoy it so much.

His response was, "Because a friend of mine kicked me in the balls."

Not quite sure what to say, and trying to maintain my composure, I responded with, "Well, I guess that took you out of commission for a while," and moved on to my next question.

Get Back to Work

One of my employees, a millwright, lives about thirty-five miles away from the plant. Keeping in mind his position, he was out running errands for the company when he was injured. He was T-boned at an intersection and was seriously hurt. He was totally disabled for the time being, and I followed the procedures and got the paperwork filled out for Workers' Compensation. Later that year, I get a call from Workers' Compensation. I had been very aggressively trying to get him modified work accommodations, and they contacted me to say that he was ready to go back to work with some limitations. "Okay," I said, "great. What are these accommodations?"

"Well, first, he can't drive a motor vehicle."

To this, I said, "Okay, no problem. I know some other employees who live close to him, and they can drive him in to work."

"The second restriction is that he cannot be a passenger in a motor vehicle." After this comment, there was dead silence for about thirty seconds.

"Okay," I responded, "to help you understand, he's a millwright, and he lives about thirty-five miles away from the plant. So how does he get to work? Am I supposed to ship large pieces of equipment to his house for him to work on there?"

Then there was dead silence from the other end, but finally the person said, "We didn't think of that. We'll have to call you back!"

What Are You Looking At?

I was in the last stages of my pregnancy and our company was being investigated for improper land utilization. The Ministry of the Environment had decided to conduct an investigation and they needed to interview the vice president in charge of shit (literally) in our company. As the lawyer, I was supposed to be present during the interview to ensure that nothing "shitty" was said that could be misconstrued.

The meeting with the ministry was scheduled on, of all days, October 31—Halloween. It was tradition at our company to all dress up in some sort of Halloween costume. With me being thirty-six weeks pregnant, what was I supposed to dress up as (aside from the I'm-carrying-a-basketball type of thing, which is so lame)? So one day I was driving back from work and I saw a sign for the restaurant called Hooters. *Wouldn't it be really cool if my belly could be the Hooters owl?* I thought. So I went home and got orange, brown, and black construction paper. I made two big circles for the owl's eyes and taped them to my breasts; I secured round, brown wings to the sides of my belly, and I had chicken feet coming out from under my tummy.

So I showed up and we were having our Halloween party and a potluck lunch. I got a call from the front desk saying that the guy from the ministry was there for the meeting. I walked in and sat down in front of the guy and he was staring at me, not knowing what to say. So I reached out with my hand to introduce myself—stating my name and that I was the lawyer at XYZ company—and he said, "Umm, what are you wearing?"

Smiling, I said, "I'm the Hooters owl."

He had problems looking at me—this pregnant woman with large breasts, dressed up as the Hooters owl, with the VP of shit by my side—and conducting this interview with a straight face.

The vice president of HR (who hadn't seen me yet) kept texting me during the meeting. She kept saying that she had to see my costume and I said, "I'm in the middle of this interview and I can't leave."

She texted back: *You are eight and a half months pregnant, damn it. Tell them you have to pee!*

To this day, the VP loves to tell the story of how I was pregnant and dressed up like the Hooters owl!

Nice Doggy

I work as a real estate agent and was showing a home to a client in a prestigious area of town. Homeowners and sellers usually say things like, "It's a friendly dog, so don't worry about it," or "The dog's name is Dash," or "Just make sure that when you open the door, you say hi to Dash." So I pushed the lockbox code and got the key in the door—and I could already see the dog in the window. This dog did not look very nice. I could see all his teeth and he was barking ferociously, so I opened the door just a crack and started saying, "Hi Dash, hi Dash, hi Dash." Dash was *not friendly at all*. I looked at my client and said, "I don't know about you, but I have no interest in seeing this place. How about you?"

She said, "Nope, I don't need to see it either."

We closed the door, locked it up, and I said, "I'm not going in there."

That same day, I was taking this same lady out to see another house. It was a hot, hot, hot summer day. For one of the last houses we went to see, the office said, "The tenant might be home." So when we got there I rang the doorbell, opened up the door, and called out, "Hello, hello, hello," but we didn't hear a thing.

We were looking at the house and making fun of it because the boys had their stuff strewn all over, and in the extreme heat, it smelled bad. We looked all through the bedrooms and finally came to one where the door was closed. Thinking we were alone, we entered—and there was a guy, *buck naked*, sleeping on the floor. I quickly closed the bedroom door and ran out. I said to my client, "Okay, so you are not buying a house today. Let's go!" Two incidents in one day! Poor woman!

Give Us a Hug

We had one lady who was selling her house because she had dementia, and I was taking a client to see the place. When we got to the house, the old lady ran out and grabbed me with her two hands. She pulled me close, grabbed my boobs, twisted them, and asked, "Are they real or fake?" She then proceeded to give me a hug. My client was standing there, horrified, while I kept asking my real estate partner, "Did that just happen? Did she just grab my boobs?" Her husband came out and apologized for his wife's behavior, stating that she wasn't well.

A week later, our office conducted a Meals on Wheels event, to provide hot and nourishing food to the elderly in our area of town. One of the agents came into the office and told me the story of this lady who grabbed her boobs, and I said, "Don't tell me!" We compared addresses, and sure enough, it was the same elderly lady. I asked my colleague, "Did she grab you like this and then give you a hug after?" and she said, "Yes, she did exactly that! Oh my God!" Apparently, she does that to all the women she meets!

Garage Door

Years and years ago, I was representing a buyer and showing him properties around town. One of the houses he liked was in an affluent area. It had a one-floor plan because, unfortunately, due to health reasons, my client couldn't do stairs anymore.

The day of the home inspection was one of the worst snowstorm days on record. I called the agent and asked if there was any way we could gain access through the garage, because the buyer wouldn't be able to navigate the stairs during that weather—it would be too slippery. The agent said, "Sure, no problem," and gave me the garage code.

I got there a few minutes early and put the lights on. The inspector showed up and started, and my client arrived in a handicapped van. So I went through the kitchen and laundry room area and opened up the garage door. It was icy, snowy, and stormy, and even the ice and the wind were blowing into the garage. I told my client to take his time.

When I opened up the laundry room door just off of the garage, the cat bolted out of the house and made a beeline for the garage door. I panicked. *They told me not to let the cat out!* I thought.

So I was watching the cat that was now outside of the garage. The garage door was slowly closing and the cat realized—and you can just imagine that the cat was thinking, *This isn't the type of weather I want to be in*. He turned around and decided to come back in but got squashed under the garage door.

Now that the cat was trapped under the garage door, I was even more panicked. I pushed the button again, but the door just went farther down. So now, instead of merely being caught, the cat was being squeezed.

I pushed the button once more—now frantic—and the door finally started coming back up. The cat was released! All I could think was, *Oh, please, God, let the cat be okay, or I am going to die.* I started yelling at the cat, "Get up! Get up! It's okay now!"

You could tell the cat was reeling, but its eyes finally opened. Then, all of a sudden, the cat did get up, but he did so really, really slowly. He went inside the house, found a little area in the kitchen, and flopped down.

We spent two and a half hours in the house, if not longer, and I kept staring at the cat. The cat did not move, but he was conscious. So I called the agent to say, "I'm at the home inspection, and I just need to tell you what happened." So I told her the whole story, and I said, "Look, I'm truly sorry and I feel terrible, but the vendors really need to know that I don't think their cat is okay, and I think I might have done damage."

I felt absolutely awful. I think I heard the next day that the vendor did find out that I did some damage to the cat but that the cat was okay. But apparently he wasn't okay for long, because he ended up dying. The good part of the story is, however, that the vendors were moving and they really didn't want to take the cat with them to the next place. So everything happens for a reason.

Best Friends

I was working for the government in a department that produced small checks for low-income seniors. Part of my job was to analyze discrepancies and confirm eligibility for this benefit payment. It was a Friday and an elderly gentleman came into the office. I was the account representative for him, so I was asked to meet with him, as he claimed to the receptionist that he hadn't received his last three checks.

When I entered the room, his first words to me were: "I was in World War II, I have shot and killed someone, and I own a gun and am not afraid to use it."

My response to him was: "I'm here to help you get your checks. If you shoot me, this will prolong the process and people in prison do not receive this benefit."

We proceeded with the meeting and I advised him that I would do an analysis of his account. I was able to fix the problem and cut him a check that day. By the end of the day, I was his best buddy and he phoned me regularly for months to let me know that his checks had arrived.

Did You Just Ask Me That?

For a couple of years, I worked as tour operator in White Horse, Yukon. The resort catered to clients who would come in from the cruise ships. We would, as a result, get a lot of interesting customers. They would ask some of the most bizarre questions. After a while, we devised some funny responses to their questions that we would deliver with perfect poker faces. Here are just a few:

How much do the mountains weigh?

8.1718E+17 tons.

(We had actually figured this out by taking the density times volume equals mass equation.)

What time do the Northern Lights come on?

The manager has the key to turn them on, but we can arrange for a wake-up call if you like.

How do y'all get the snow on top of the mountains?

Oh, that's not snow; we direct the birds to poo on top of it.

Can I Go Now?

I worked for a large insurance company as the director of human resources. We were hiring for a sales and marketing vice president, and my boss wanted me to meet with the recruitment firm he wanted to use. So off I went downtown.

As soon as I arrived at the address, I thought there must have been a mistake. The building was really run-down on the outside, and as soon as I entered it, I noticed a really horrid smell. I called my assistant to verify the address and she confirmed that, yes, this was the place. So I got on the elevator and pressed the button to go up.

As I walked through the halls, I was disgusted to see the paint peeling and to smell an odor emanating from the torn and ripped carpet. I reached the office and opened the door, only to be visually bombarded with all sorts of stuff. There were paintings, sculptures, and *things* all over the office, including (and this made me jump at first) a lifelike dummy sitting in the corner of the room. I tried to absorb the room's details, but it was like being visually attacked. There wasn't one square inch of this office that didn't have stuff all over. I realized that I'd been standing there for a couple of minutes when someone came out to greet me. He said he was the owner's assistant and that the owner would be out shortly. He told me to make myself at home. I thought, *That's impossible in a place like this,* but I found myself a chair and sat down.

Another five minutes went by. The owner walked out, introduced himself, and asked how I liked the reception area. Never in my whole life have I wanted to maintain a poker face as I did in that moment. I nodded and smiled, and we walked into his office—which looked like a visual desert after the reception area. He then proceeded to tell me that he had been watching me via a video camera, since he had certain religious artifacts and pictures in his lobby. He said he could tell what religion visitors were by the artifacts they looked at.

Oh, it gets better.

He then told me how he sources candidates out. He finds out everything about them: where they live, what their background is, how many kids they have, and what type of relationship they have with their wives or husbands. He winked at me as he made this last statement, and said, "I even find out how good their sex life is."

At that point, I wanted to run out of there and take a long hot shower. He went on and on and on about how good he was, how good his agency was, *blah, blah, blah*. He then started asking about me, and I quickly turned the conversation back to him and listened for another nauseating twenty-five minutes. *I have to get out of here,* I thought, so I looked at my watch and exclaimed that I had to leave in order to catch the train. I couldn't wait to escape.

The next day, my boss came in and asked, smiling, "How was it? Did you like the guy?" I told him my initial impressions and my concerns from a legal standpoint, to which he replied that he had a longstanding relationship with this guy and that this was the firm we were going to go with— end of story.

Who Took My Shoes?

My husband, mother-in-law, and I run a seasonal campground in northern Ontario. Our place is surrounded by beautiful trees, a big lake, birds, and a real variety of animals. The air is fresh, and every morning we look forward to what kind of adventure our environment will bring. The saying that we have adopted over the years is: "Anything can happen at _____! There's never a dull moment!" Of course, we say this with enthusiasm and a smirk on our faces! Many of our park occupants are full-timers and what I would like to call jokers. One day last summer, one of them came into the office with a real concern.

He explained to me how this fox would come to his trailer during the night, steal his shoes, sandals, his kids' shoes, and so forth. In fact, he couldn't leave anything outside; it was all being taken.

My initial reaction was to laugh; I knew this guy, and he regularly liked to yank on my chain, so I thought he was joking. But the next day, to our surprise, another park occupant came in to complain about the same thing—that *his* shoes and sandals were going missing!

Later that week, we were hiking, and—lo and behold—we found a pile of shoes and sandals (no matching pairs!) in the woods near our trail!

Now, everybody knows to keep all shoes and sandals *inside* the trailer at night!

What's Wrong with That?

I worked in a staffing company and was about six months into my job when I got a call that still makes me shake my head when I think about it. The woman who called was one of my customers and someone with whom I had worked closely for the previous six months. When she began speaking, she seemed really hesitant to talk with me, which was weird because we had established a really good working relationship. After a few minutes of her trying to beat around the bush, I finally said, "Look. We've been working together for a while now. If there's a problem with a staff member, then I need to be aware of it so I can fix whatever the issue is." She then asked me how much we paid our employees. Now, normally we don't divulge these figures, but in this case—because of the large contract that we had with them and the transparent relationship we shared—I told her, but I added, "Why is this important?"

She then said, "You'll understand when I share this story with you." She then told me that she had seen one of our employees working on the corner in the financial district, downtown.

"Was he having lunch?" I asked.

"No, he was dressed as a bum," she replied.

You could have heard a pin drop on the line. I finally asked, "*What?*"

"He was dressed like a bum, with a hat in front of him and a sign begging for money."

"Are you sure it was him?" I asked.

"Yes, absolutely—because of his mole."

Now, this employee had a rather distinguishing mole on his face, so I asked again whether she was sure. "Absolutely," she answered. So I told her that I would call the employee in and get to the bottom of this. "Keep me posted," she responded.

So I arranged to have the employee come in to meet with me. I agonized over this meeting all afternoon and evening. The next morning, the employee walked into our office dressed to the nines, wearing a sharp suit, great shoes, and so on. As I walked into the reception area and saw him, I kept thinking this couldn't possibly be true. I escorted him back to my office and started right in:

"I don't know how else to start this other than to jump right in. Our client, who you have been working with for the past month, thought she saw you on the corner of ___ and ___, dressed as a bum and begging for money." I paused and looked right at him, and his response still haunts me to this day.

"Yup. That was me," he said. He shifted in his seat and smiled at me.

This was not the scenario I had anticipated, so I was aghast. "You mean to say that it was *you* and that, during your lunch hour, you dressed as a bum and went begging for money?"

He smiled again and said, "Yes, I have been doing this for the past several years. How else do you think I can afford to buy these suits and shoes and go away on holiday so often?"

Still shocked, I asked him, "But don't you find anything wrong with begging for money when you clearly have the smarts to get a decent-paying job?"

He started laughing. "Do you think what you pay me is a decent wage?"

I responded, "I know your file and background. You have a master's degree in finance, and we put you to work with one of our larger clients in the financial district because of where it could lead you in your career. You do realize that you've blown it, right? I am pulling you off the assignment, and I will be asking my boss to put you on the do-not-use-anymore list."

"Fine," he said, standing up and straightening out his tie. "I will simply find another agency to work with."

I stood up and walked up to him, so that I was standing about five inches away from his face. "It's a small town and people talk," I said. "Even competitors communicate, and even if that doesn't make you understand that what you are doing is wrong, I know that karma will." He laughed as he left.

We did end up putting him on that list, and when my boss called around to some agencies, it turned out that he had done this before to several others in the industry. To this day, I'm shocked when I think of his response and his complete lack of remorse over his actions.

Temps

I worked in a very large and reputable staffing agency, and some of our applicants would continually surprise us with stunts they pulled on the job. These are just a few of them. We had one employee who needed to do yoga poses on her desk. Every half hour, she would clear the papers off her desk and proceed to do complex poses—to stay nimble, as she later explained. We had another employee whose pastime during downtime at work was to practice his drawing skills; specifically, he would draw the people around him naked. Unfortunately, he wasn't careful, and one afternoon he left his booklet open on his desk. We had another employee who very much disliked the position that she was in, but had never told us. We got a call from one of our clients who said he had found a ten-page letter filled with crass remarks and awful sentiments toward everyone in the office that she had dealings with. She left it on her desk the last day of the assignment. We had another who was brilliant on every one of her assignments, but she would constantly brag about the connections she had. She once told us that she had worked for the CIA and the FBI and was such personal friends with the president that she could call him up right away and have lunch with him. Despite her stories, we never once received any complaints about her work habits.

The Judge

One summer, I worked at an electronics shop near the courthouse downtown. One day, a gentleman came in dressed in a judge's robe. He looked very stately and spoke quite well, and when it came time to make his purchases, he produced a check that had the name and contacts for the courthouse on it. Yet there was something about this guy that made us doubt that he was truly a judge. So when he left we called the courthouse and asked if this guy existed and would be paying with a courthouse check. We were told in no uncertain terms that *no*, not only did this guy not exist but no one wrote checks from the courthouse for purchases like the ones he had just made. At that time I was quite fit, so off I ran from the store to catch up to this guy. After running a couple of blocks, I saw him walk into a local bar. I went in, just as the cops were pulling up to the bar. I grabbed him while he just sat there looking so calm in his judge's robe with his purchases beside him. We found out later that he had done this before. Fast-forward a couple of months, and I was called in to act as a witness at his hearing. Before the judge pronounced his sentence, though, he reamed into the guy. "Of all things to impersonate, a *judge*? Do you realize how hard we have to work to gain trust in the community?" The most interesting part is I could still picture the guy in his judge's robe, and now here was the real judge delivering his sentence.

I Did Not Know That

I work as a hairdresser. One day, I was ready to color a client's hair when she suddenly felt very faint. I obviously took that very seriously and she admitted that she had not eaten since the previous weekend. It was Wednesday of the following week, so I asked her if she was on a spiritual or medical fast, but she said no—she was trying to lose twenty pounds by the weekend. I thought that was bizarre, especially because of the message that would send to her teenage daughter, who was sitting nearby. So I said to her, "We need to get you something to eat."

Unfortunately, at our location we don't have anything like a grocery store nearby, so I said to my assistant, "Can you go and get some juice? Don't get anything acidic—just something like peach juice that won't upset her stomach and some natural yogurt."

My client stopped me, however, and said to my assistant, "No, I want a Diet Coke and a Mars bar."

I said to the client, "I'm not sure if that's the best way to recoup after a four-day fast—especially if you're trying to lose weight."

"Well, you obviously don't know anything about nutrition," she replied.

"I would kind of like to think that I *do* know something about it," I countered.

She said, "Well, everybody knows that, if you eat a Mars bar and drink a Diet Coke at the same time, the Diet Coke eats and neutralizes the calories of the Mars bar."

I looked at her and said, "I did not know that." I glanced over at my assistant and asked her, "Please, go get this lady a Mars bar and a Diet Coke." I know one thing, though: the lady didn't lose that twenty pounds by the weekend.

Green Men

I had another client who told me that he firmly believed we couldn't possibly be *the only people out there*.

I said, "Well, I don't believe it."

He replied, "Well, you are going to look pretty silly and embarrassed when the Little Green Men arrive."

I told him that the day the Little Green Men arrived, no one would be embarrassed because we'd be too busy panicking.

Your most unhappy customers are your greatest source of learning.
—Bill Gates

Sandbox Treasures

1. I guess I was wrong; not everyone knows basic nutrition.
2. Your actions will eventually catch up with you. Not everyone who begs, however, is deceitful.
3. Wow, really? *Little Green Men*, you say.
4. Halloween costumes and business meetings make for great stories.
5. There are some questions that should never be asked during an interview.

Conclusion

Who knew that you could learn so much about yourself while writing a book about other people's stories? When I began this endeavor, my book coach tried to warn me that the process of writing would transform me. A dear friend of mine, who wrote *With the Stroke of a Pen,* tried to tell me the same thing. I guess that old adage rings true—that you never know something until you experience it yourself.

I learned *four important lessons* writing this book:

1. That you have to ask for *help*. (There is no shame in it. After all, we were always told as children to stick together and hold hands while crossing the street. At what age do we start thinking we have to do it all on our own?)
2. That the things we *believe* about ourselves are often ideas we inherit from our families. Very often, they no longer hold true.
3. That sharing *stories* with each other helps us heal and connect through shared experiences.
4. That *mental health* affects so many of us, and until we can truly share our experiences and have an open dialogue around this issue, things won't change for the better.

In writing *Welcome to My Sandbox,* I realized that I hadn't challenged the things I believed about myself—ever. In the process of compiling the stories in this book, I had to face my relationship with success, failure, money, strength, personal power, and perseverance. I started redefining my own story and creating new ones with happier endings—ones that better described the me that *is* versus the me that *was*. Don't get me wrong; the story of my past will never change, but its power over me has and will continue to.

I watched as person after person who shared a story with me was transformed by the experience. Having people stop and listen—with care, compassion, and shared laughter, of course—was a wonderful experience both for them and for me. We need to start sharing and listening to one another's stories. We learn through storytelling, and we are transformed by sharing our tales. When people let us know that our story made a difference to them, our experiences are endowed with a special value and a deeper resonance.

I really enjoyed listening to and reading everyone's stories. In fact, these tales confirmed what I have known for a very long time in HR. It isn't a complicated equation: if you hire people with great attitudes and provide them with a fun and engaging working environment, the returns will be there. Your ROI (return on investment) for the lower absenteeism and turnover rates—and heightened creativity and innovation—will be noticeable. Perhaps it is that simple.

There wasn't a single person—not even one—with whom I shared my reasons for writing this book who wasn't also affected, in one way or another, by mental health. I heard stories of daughters who were impacted by their mothers' mental health issues, and who were acting as caregivers to their families while their parents were in shock therapy. I heard from other sisters who had lost their brothers through suicide, and from mothers and fathers who had to—and who continue to—deal with mental health issues in their families. Mental health issues are more prevalent than we know, and it is time we start sharing our stories so we can change the way mental health is viewed and dealt with in our society.

I truly hope that you enjoyed reading everyone's stories; I sure had a lot of fun putting this book together.

If you have a story that you would like to share, or an idea for another book of stories, then I encourage you to write me at:

story@welcometomysandbox.com

I am currently gathering stories from military and police services, to honor those who have served and continue to serve. As with all of the *Welcome to My Sandbox* series, a portion of the proceeds from this particular book will be given to organizations that provide mental health assistance to those who have served.

I am blessed in many ways. I not only get to follow my passion of being an author and speaker, but I also get to work with amazing clients and ensure that "people play nice in the sandbox" with my full-time business: Fluidhr. If you would like to learn more about the why, the what, and the how I do what I do, then please visit the company website at:

www.fluidhr.ca

After nourishment, shelter, and companionship, stories are the thing we need most in the world.
—Philip Pullman

Here's to laughter, to sharing, and to making the world a better place, one story at a time!